S0-CAD-729

BE HEALTHY
BE SLIM

Managing Editor Catherine Saxelby
Editor, Diane Hodges
Food Editor Sheryle Eastwood
Assistant Food Editor Rachel Blackmore
Editor Marian Broderick
Editorial Coordinator Margaret Kelly

PHOTOGRAPHY AND STYLING
Yanto Noerianto
Michelle Gorry
Andrew Elton

DESIGN AND PRODUCTION
Sheridan Carter
Monica Kessler-Tay
Chris Hatcher

Publisher
Philippa Sandall

Cover - Kim Alexis and her son Jamie.
Clothes by Danskin.
Photograph by Mark Babushkin.
Styled by Laura McCarthy and Bianco Borges Henry.
Hair and makeup by Steven Jones for Vicki Cole.
Designed by Michelle Wiener.

Published by J.B. Fairfax Press Inc., a wholly owned
subsidiary of J.B. Fairfax International

© J.B. Fairfax Press Inc., 1990

This book is copyright. Apart from any fair dealing for
the purpose of private study, research, criticism or
review, as permitted under the Copyright Act, no part
may be reproduced by any process without the
written permission of the publisher. Enquiries should
be made in writing to the publisher.

Be Healthy Be Slim
Includes Index
ISBN 1 56197 003 4

Printed In Singapore By Toppan Printing.

CHECK-AND-GO

When planning a meal, use the easy Check-and-Go boxes which appear beside each ingredient. Simply check on your pantry shelf and if the ingredients are not there, tick the boxes as a reminder to add those items to your shopping list. To save time for busy cooks, ingredients have been kept to a minimum in all recipes and, where possible, convenience products used.

CONTENTS

BE HEALTHY
BE SLIM

Good food and enjoyable meals are truly one of life's great pleasures. Yet today, with the multitude of diet books and food "scares" that regularly appear in the media, food has become a source of concern and unhappiness for many people. This book aims to counter the myths and fallacies surrounding food, dieting and nutrition. It is not just for people who are watching their weight, but also for anyone interested in healthy eating.
All recipes are low in fat, low in sugar, with no added salt. And they will give your meals a boost of all-important fiber, nature's own appetite supressant.
Not only are they good for you and your waistline, they are also delicious, quick and easy to prepare, and suitable for all the family. When you're eating our dishes, you won't feel as if you're on a diet! Each recipe has a nutritional analysis, so you can see exactly how many calories, fiber, cholesterol and fat you are eating.
Because weight control is more than just a diet plan, we've included information on nutrition, exercise, body shape, latest research on obesity, eating out and help for overweight children. There is also a fat counter of common foods, as cutting down fats (including polyunsaturated fats) is currently considered the best way to stay slim and healthy.
If you don't want to give up your favorite dishes, look for our tips on how to adapt recipes to be lower in fat, cholesterol and salt.

MEASURING UP

For measuring ingredients in our recipes we have used a nest of metric measuring cups and a set of metric measuring spoons. All cup and spoon measures are level.

METRIC MEASURES

Cups

$1/4$ cup	60 mL
$1/3$ cup	80 mL
$1/2$ cup	125 mL
1 cup	250 mL

Spoons

$1/4$ teaspoon	1.25 mL
$1/2$ teaspoon	2.5 mL
1 teaspoon	5 mL
1 tablespoon	20 mL

QUICK CONVERTER

g	oz	mL	fl.oz
30	1	30	1
60	2	60	2
125	4	125	4
250	8	250	8
370	12	370	12
500	16	500	16

FISH AND
SEAFOOD

These fabulous fish and seafood recipes will show you how appetizing and enjoyable food that is good for you can be.

❖
MUSSELS IN WINE AND GARLIC

Serves 4

- ☐ **2 teaspoons olive oil**
- ☐ **2 cloves garlic, crushed**
- ☐ **4 green onions, chopped**
- ☐ **1 stalk celery, chopped**
- ☐ **1 carrot, chopped**
- ☐ **1 teaspoon whole black peppercorns**
- ☐ **1 teaspoon chopped fresh basil leaves**
- ☐ **¹/₂ teaspoon dried rosemary leaves**
- ☐ **1 bay leaf**
- ☐ **1 cup dry white wine**
- ☐ **2 pounds mussels, scrubbed and bearded**
- ☐ **14-ounce can peeled tomatoes, undrained and mashed**
- ☐ **¹/₂ teaspoon sugar**

1 Heat oil in a large saucepan. Cook garlic, geen onions, celery and carrot for 2-3 minutes. Stir in peppercorns, basil, rosemary, bay leaf and wine. Bring to boiling, then reduce heat and simmer for 10 minutes.
2 Strain liquid and discard vegetables. Return liquid to the pan and bring back to boiling. Add mussels, tomatoes and sugar. Cover and cook over medium heat for 6 minutes.
3 Remove cover and discard any unopened mussels. Arrange remaining mussels in serving bowls and keep warm. Boil liquid for 5-6 minutes longer, or until it reduces slightly and thickens. Spoon sauce over mussels and serve.

300 calories per serving

Fat	7.1 g	low
Cholesterol	250 mg	high
Fiber	2.1 g	medium
Sodium	585 mg	high

NUTRITION TIP

Shellfish is often avoided because of its high cholesterol content. But it is not as rich as was once believed. Apart from shrimp, all shellfish contain low to moderate levels. Shrimp rate the highest in cholesterol, followed by lobster, crab and mussels. Scallops, oysters and octopus are very low, less than lean meats or even chicken.

❖
STIR-FRY HONEY-GINGER SHRIMP

Serves 4

- ☐ **2 tablespoons polyunsaturated oil**
- ☐ **6 green onions, chopped**
- ☐ **1-2 fresh red chilies, seeded and sliced**
- ☐ **2 cloves garlic, crushed**
- ☐ **1 teaspoon grated fresh ginger**
- ☐ **2 pounds shrimp, peeled and deveined**
- ☐ **2 teaspoons cornstarch blended with ¹/₂ cup water**
- ☐ **2 teaspoons low-salt soy sauce**
- ☐ **1 tablespoon honey**
- ☐ **14-ounce jar baby corn, drained**

1 Heat oil in a frypan or wok. Stir-fry green onions and chilies for 1-2 minutes. Toss in garlic, ginger and shrimp and stir-fry 3-4 minutes longer, until shrimp turn pink.
2 Combine cornstarch mixture, soy sauce and honey. Add cornstarch mixture and corn to shrimp mixture. Stir-fry for 2-3 minutes, or until sauce boils and thickens. Spoon onto dinner plates and serve immediately.

482 calories per serving

Fat	11.1 g	medium
Cholesterol	500 mg	high
Fiber	5.5 g	high
Sodium	1090 mg	high

❖
MARINATED FISH SALAD

Serves 4

- ☐ **1 cup lemon juice**
- ☐ **1 cup lime juice**
- ☐ **4 tablespoons finely chopped fresh coriander**
- ☐ **4 firm white fish fillets**
- ☐ **lettuce leaves**
- ☐ **1 onion, sliced into rings**
- ☐ **14-ounce can mandarin orange segments, drained**

DRESSING

- ☐ **1 teaspoon grated fresh ginger**
- ☐ **1 small fresh red chili, seeded and finely chopped**
- ☐ **1 clove garlic, crushed**
- ☐ **1 tablespoon polyunsaturated oil**
- ☐ **freshly ground black pepper**

1 Combine lemon juice, lime juice and coriander in a shallow glass dish. Add fish; cover and refrigerate for 3-4 hours, turning occasionally.
2 To make dressing, place ginger, chili, garlic, oil and pepper in a screwtop jar and shake to combine.
3 Arrange lettuce leaves on serving platter. Drain fish and arrange on lettuce leaves. Pour dressing over and top with onion rings and orange segments.

210 calories per serving

Fat	4.7 g	low
Cholesterol	79 mg	low
Fiber	1.3 g	medium
Sodium	171 mg	low

COOK'S TIP

You will find that the fish turns opaque after marinating in citrus juices, because of the acidity of the juices. Try to eat fish at least two to three times a week. Fish is an excellent food, high in protein, vitamins and minerals, but low in fat and cholesterol. Our marinated fish salad is ideal for weight watchers and cholesterol watchers alike.

From top clockwise:
Mussels in Wine and Garlic,
Stir-Fry Honey-Ginger Shrimp
and Marinated Fish Salad

❖
TERIYAKI FISH

Serves 4

- ☐ **4 large firm white fish fillets**
- ☐ **2 teaspoons sesame seeds**

MARINADE
- ☐ **3 tablespoons teriyaki sauce**
- ☐ **1 tablespoon honey**
- ☐ **1 tablespoon dry sherry**
- ☐ **$\frac{1}{4}$ teaspoon grated fresh ginger**
- ☐ **1 clove garlic, crushed**

1   Place fish fillets in a single layer in a shallow dish. To make marinade, combine teriyaki sauce, honey, sherry, ginger and garlic and pour over fish. Cover and marinate for 1 hour.

2   Toss sesame seeds in a frying pan and cook over medium heat until golden brown, stirring frequently.

3   Remove fish from marinade and grill for 2-3 minutes on each side. Baste occasionally with marinade during cooking. Serve sprinkled with sesame seeds.

270 calories per serving

Fat	5.6 g	low
Cholesterol	158 mg	medium
Fiber	0.1 g	low
Sodium	516 mg	high

Teriyaki Fish

COOK'S TIP
Fish cooks very quickly under the grill. Remember to turn halfway through cooking time. For best results, preheat the grill and marinate or lightly oil the fish or kebabs. The heat of the grill and the thickness of the fish will determine cooking time.

Fish Tips

Be healthy and slim with fish. Try the following suggestions to create dishes to suit you and your family's taste.

ON THE BARBECUE

When barbecuing fish, be sure not to overcook or the fish will be dry and tough. As with all fish cooking, the fish should just flake when tested with a fork. Dampen the coals with water during cooking to reduce heat. This will also keep the fish moist. The cooking time will vary depending on the heat of the fire and the thickness of the fish. To add an interesting flavor to barbecued food, place sprigs of rosemary or thyme on the coals. This also works well using lemon or orange peel.

✧ To cook a whole fish, squeeze lemon juice into the cavity of the fish and fill with lemon slices and sprigs of dill, mint or herbs of your choice. Wrap in two layers of foil and cook on the barbecue for 25-30 minutes or until fish just flakes.

✧ Squeeze lemon juice over fish steaks or fillets before cooking. Top with slices of tomato, peppers, onions and mushrooms, season liberally with freshly ground black pepper. Wrap in two layers of foil and cook on the barbecue for 20-30 minutes or until fish just flakes.

✧ Kebabs make wonderful barbecue food. They can be prepared in advance and cooked when you are ready. Use a firm-fleshed white fish (halibut, cod), cut into 1-inch cubes and marinated in a mixture of wine or cider, fresh herbs and freshly ground black pepper for 20 minutes. Thread fish cubes and vegetables of your choice onto lightly oiled bamboo skewers. Barbecue for 5-10 minutes

✧ Shrimps are great cooked on the barbecue. Shell and devein, then marinate in a mixture of tomato juice, wine or stock, garlic and freshly ground black pepper. Thread onto lightly greased bamboo skewers and cook on the barbecue for 10-15 minutes or until the shrimp change color.

UNDER THE HEAT

✧ To broil a whole fish, make several cuts on either side of the fish. Combine 2 tablespoons olive oil, $1/2$ teaspoon ground cumin, $1/2$ teaspoon ground coriander and a pinch of chili powder; brush over fish and broil for 5 minutes each side, or until fish just flakes.

IN THE MICROWAVE

Cooking fish in the microwave is quick and easy and there are no fishy smells in the kitchen after cooking.

✧ To cook fish steaks or fillets, place in a shallow microwave-safe dish, sprinkle with 2-3 tablespoons of lemon juice and freshly chopped herbs. Cover and microwave on HIGH (100%) for 4-5 minutes per pound.

✧ To poach fish, place fillets or steaks in a shallow microwave-safe dish, pour over wine, stock or a mixture of wine and stock and season with freshly ground black pepper and herbs of your choice. Cover and cook on HIGH (100%) for 5 minutes per pound.

✧ To cook a whole fish, fill the cavity with orange slices and sprigs of fennel. Place on a large microwave-safe dish, cover and microwave on MEDIUM-HIGH (70%) for 5 minutes per pound.

❖
LEMON FISH PARCELS

Serves 4

- ☐ **4 large white fish fillets**
- ☐ **1 tablespoon finely chopped capers**
- ☐ **$1/2$ cup lemon juice**
- ☐ **freshly ground black pepper**
- ☐ **8 asparagus spears (fresh or canned)**
- ☐ **$1/2$ teaspoon paprika**

1   Lightly grease four sheets of aluminum foil and place a fish fillet in the center of each sheet.

2   Top each fillet with a teaspoon of capers. Pour over lemon juice and season with pepper. Place two asparagus spears over each fillet and dust lightly with paprika.

3   Fold up edges of aluminum foil and completely encase fish. Place parcels on an oven tray and bake at 350° for 15-20 minutes, or until fish flakes when tested with a fork. Remove from parcels to serve.

125 calories per serving

Fat	*2.7 g*	*low*
Cholesterol	*79 mg*	*low*
Fiber	*0.4 g*	*low*
Sodium	*218 mg*	*low*

Lemon Fish Parcels

CLASSIC LIGHT

SPANISH GARLIC SHRIMP

A gourmet delight made lighter and healthier for today.

Serves 6 as an entrée or 4 as a light luncheon dish.

- ☐ 1¹/₂ **tablespoons butter**
- ☐ **1 tablespoon polyunsaturated oil**
- ☐ **8 cloves garlic, crushed**
- ☐ **6 green onions, chopped**
- ☐ **1 small red chili, seeded and chopped**
- ☐ **14-ounce can peeled tomatoes, undrained and mashed**
- ☐ **2 pounds shrimp, deveined, with tails intact**

1 Heat butter and oil in a frying pan. Cook garlic, green onions and chili for 1-2 minutes. Stir in tomatoes and cook over medium heat until boiling.

2 Divide shrimp between four individual ovenproof dishes. Spoon tomato mixture over and bake at 400° for 10-15 minutes, or until shrimp turn pink.

348 calories per serving

Fat	11.1 g	medium
Cholesterol	512 mg	high
Fiber	2.2 g	medium
Sodium	1091 mg	high

HOW WE'VE CUT FAT AND CALORIES

Garlic shrimp are usually cooked and served in lots of butter and olive oil.

✧ To reduce fat, we cooked ours in just a little butter for taste plus 1 tablespoon oil.

✧ We added flavor with green onions, garlic and chili in a spicy tomato concasse which created a light, delicious dish with plenty of sauce.

✧ There is no need for salt when you can make imaginative use of garlic, herbs and spices.

HOW TO ADAPT
YOUR RECIPES

LIMITING FAT

Grill, dry-roast, stir-fry, microwave, casserole or poach in stock. A non-stick frying pan or "dry frying pan" with a tight-fitting lid is a must for low-fat cookery. Also look for silicon-coated paper pan liners which line your frying pan and transfer the heat to food direct – no fat needed at all!

• To brown meat or vegetables, brush your pan with oil (don't pour it in) and cook over moderate heat to avoid sticking.

• Use small quantities of butter, margarine, oil, cream, mayonnaise and cooking fats.

• Substitute low-fat dairy foods for full-cream products. Low-fat unflavored yogurt makes an excellent substitute for cream (do not boil after adding it). Use fat-reduced and skim milks instead of full-cream milk and ricotta, cottage cheese and fat-reduced cheeses for regular cheeses.

• Offer substitutes for whipped cream on puddings – low-fat ice cream, vanilla custard, thick unflavored yogurt, or a blend of ricotta and yogurt flavored with vanilla extract and lemon rind.

INCREASING FIBER INTAKE

Where possible, do not peel vegetables, but cook with the skin on.

• Try brown rice more often. It adds an interesting nutty flavor. Try buckwheat and barley, two high-fiber grains.

• Add cooked or canned soy beans or kidney beans to casseroles; throw a handful of lentils into soups.

• For coatings or toppings use wholewheat bread crumbs and crushed wheat biscuits (breakfast biscuits). Alternatively, try oat bran or a mixture of oat and wheat brans.

REDUCING SALT

Don't use salt in cooking. Experiment with herbs and spices as seasoning and your palate will gradually adapt the "real" flavor of foods, which are often masked by salt. Double quantities of garlic, onion, chili, basil, dill, lemon juice lift the flavor.

• Salt substitutes (potassium chloride or a mixture of salt and potassium chloride) are helpful. Use low-salt and salt-free food products from the supermarket. Over 50% of sodium intake comes from commercial foods like bread, butter, margarine, cheese, and luncheon meats which do not taste "salty." Stock cubes or powder, soy sauce, meat seasonings, garlic salt, Worcestershire and similar sauces all add salt.

LIMITING SUGAR

Gradually reduce the quantity of sugar and honey that you use.

BEFORE

PORK WITH TARRAGON

Serves 4

4 pork chops, about 6 ounces each
4 tablespoons all-purpose flour
1 teaspoon salt
freshly ground black pepper
4 tablespoons butter
1 onion, chopped
1/2 cup dry white wine
1/2 cup chicken stock
1 tablespoon all-purpose flour
1 cup cream
3 tablespoons fresh chopped or 3 teaspoons
dried tarragon

1   Coat pork with seasoned flour. Heat butter in a skillet and brown chops, turning each until golden in color. Transfer to a shallow casserole and keep warm. Reduce heat to low.
2   Reduce heat in skillet to low. Add onion and cook for 2-3 minutes. Add wine and stock; pour over pork. Cover and simmer for 30 minutes, or until pork is cooked.
3   Remove pork. Mix flour with a little cream until smooth and stir into casserole with remaining cream and tarragon. Pour sauce over pork and serve.

AFTER

PORK WITH TARRAGON

Serves 4

2 lean pork fillets, about 8 ounces each or 4 pork medallions, fat removed
a little all-purpose flour
freshly ground black pepper
1 tablespoon oil
1 onion, chopped
1/2 cup dry white wine
1/2 cup homemade chicken stock, without fat
2 tablespoons fresh or 1/2 teaspoon dried tarragon
1 tablespoon all-purpose flour
3 tablespoons cream
1/2 cup thick all-purpose yogurt
1 tablespoon fresh chopped tarragon (extra)

1   Combine pork with seasoned flour. Place in a greased baking dish and bake in a moderate oven 350° for 15 minutes, until just cooked.
2   Heat oil in a small saucepan and cook onion for 1-2 minutes or until golden. Add wine, stock and tarragon; cook for another 1-2 minutes, scraping side of pan.
3   Mix flour with cream until smooth and stir into pan with yogurt (do not boil). Keep warm until needed.
4   To serve, slice pork fillet and place 3-4 rounds on each plate. Spoon a little sauce over each serve and garnish with extra tarragon.

ADD FLAVOR WITH
HERBS & SPICES

There are many flavor-packed ingredients with little or no calories which you can use to improve the flavor of a dish. Garlic, lemon rind, curry powder and soy sauce are familiar examples, as well as aromatic herbs (both fresh and dried). Start using these in place of butter, cream, bacon and other high-fat ingredients, which often feature in traditional cookery. If you're cutting back on salt, herbs and spices become even more important. Fresh and pure dried herbs and spices contain virtually no sodium (salt chemically is sodium chloride), but be sure to check the label of herb mixtures. Some, such as "celery salt", "garlic salt" or "herb seasoning" often contain salt as an ingredient.

ENHANCE THE FLAVOR OF YOUR FAVORITE FOODS

Fish Bay leaf, chives, dill, fennel, horseradish, oregano, parsley tarragon

Chicken, turkey Garlic, pepper, rosemary, sage, tarragon, thyme

Beef, veal Cumin, garlic, horseradish, marjoram, oregano, pepper, thyme

Lamb, mutton Coriander, mint, rosemary, sorrel

Pork Savory, ginger, caraway, paprika, garlic, sage, thyme

Vegetables Basil, borage, caraway, chervil, chives, coriander, fennel, dill, garlic. mint, mustard, nasturtium, oregano, parsley, pepper, sage, savory, thyme

Eggs Basil, caraway, chervil, chives, sage

Fruit Allspice, anise, cinnamon, cloves, ginger, nutmeg, vanilla

MORE ABOUT HERBS

Fresh herbs can be dried or frozen for winter use.

Basil, thyme, marjoram and nasturtium can be used as a pepper substitute.

Herbs can be used to replace salt intake: try lovage, thyme and marjoram.

Scatter edible flowers over salads: marigolds, nasturtiums and the blue flowers of borage all look fantastic used this way.

Fresh herbs should be chopped only at the last moment so that the full flavor of the aromatic oils is captured in the dish. Basil and savory are a boon to people on low-salt diets.

Fresh is best. Many fresh herbs such as caraway, chervil, lemon balm, savory and sorrel are not readily available from the local fruit and vegetable market cut can all be grown easily and quickly in your garden or on the kitchen windowsill.

Chives

Caraway seed

Chinese five-spice

Horseradish

Nutmeg

Bay leaves

Cinnamon

Cloves

Parsley

Chilies

Rosemary

Dill

Basil

Mushrooms

Lemon rind, orange rind

Coriander (cilantro)

Chilies

Mint

LEAN MEAT AND
POULTRY

These mouthwatering lean meat and poultry recipes are full of delectable herbs, spices and other tantalizing ingredients that will keep you looking good and feeling better.

❖
SPICED APRICOT CHICKEN

Serves 6

- ☐ **27-ounce can apricots in natural juice, drained, juice reserved**
- ☐ **1 small red chili, seeded and finely chopped**
- ☐ **2 teaspoons ground cumin**
- ☐ **2 teaspoons ground coriander**
- ☐ **$1/2$ teaspoon curry powder**
- ☐ **1 teaspoon ground turmeric**
- ☐ **2 teaspoons grated lemon rind**
- ☐ **3 tablespoons coconut milk**
- ☐ **1 tablespoon polyunsaturated oil**
- ☐ **2 onions, chopped**
- ☐ **2 cloves garlic, crushed**
- ☐ **1 teaspoon grated fresh ginger**
- ☐ **2-pound chicken, skinned**
- ☐ **8 ounces low-fat plain yogurt**

1   Set aside six apricots. Place remaining apricots, reserved juice, chili, cumin, coriander, curry powder, turmeric, lemon rind and coconut milk in a food processor and blend until smooth.

2   Heat oil in a skillet. Cook onions, garlic and ginger for 2-3 minutes. Add chicken pieces and brown well on each side. Pour apricot purée over chicken and cook, uncovered, over low heat for 45-50 minutes or until chicken is tender.

3   Chop reserved apricots and combine with yogurt. Serve with chicken.

366 calories per serving

Fat	*16.0 g*	*medium*
Cholesterol	*116 mg*	*medium*
Fiber	*5.7 g*	*high*
Sodium	*158 mg*	*low*

NUTRITION TIP
Avoid deep-frying and roasting in fat. Instead grill, dry-roast, stir-fry, microwave, casserole or poach meat and chicken. If meat requires browning, brush pan with oil (don't pour it in) and cook quickly over high heat to seal in juices.

COOK'S TIP
When stir-frying meat, cook over medium-high heat only until meat changes color. Then add vegetables and liquid and complete the cooking. If using more than 1 pound of meat, cook in batches.

❖
CHINESE BEEF WITH SNOW PEAS

Serves 4

- ☐ **1 tablespoon polyunsaturated oil**
- ☐ **1 onion, cut into eighths**
- ☐ **1 clove garlic, crushed**
- ☐ **1 teaspoon grated fresh ginger**
- ☐ **$1/2$ pound snow peas, trimmed**
- ☐ **1 pound lean rump steak, cut into thin strips**
- ☐ **$1/2$ red pepper, sliced**

SAUCE

- ☐ **3 tablespoons dry white wine**
- ☐ **1 tablespoon low-salt soy sauce**
- ☐ **2 teaspoons cornstarch blended with 4 tablespoons beef stock**

1   Heat 2 teaspoons oil in a skillet or wok. Stir-fry onion, garlic and ginger for 2-3 minutes. Toss in snow peas and stir-fry for 2-3 minutes longer. Remove from pan and set aside.

2   Heat remaining oil in pan and stir-fry meat and pepper until meat changes color and is just cooked through.

3   To make sauce, combine wine, soy sauce and cornstarch mixture. Pour over meat in pan and cook until sauce boils and thickens. Reduce heat and return vegetables to pan. Stir-fry for 1-2 minutes to heat through.

294 calories per serving

Fat	*10.8 g*	*medium*
Cholesterol	*103 mg*	*medium*
Fiber	*1.5 g*	*medium*
Sodium	*163 mg*	*low*

❖
VEAL IN TWO-PEPPERCORN SAUCE

Serves 6

- ☐ **2 teaspoons olive oil**
- ☐ **6 lean veal schnitzels**
- ☐ **$1/2$ cup evaporated skim milk**
- ☐ **2 tablespoons port**
- ☐ **1 teaspoon canned green peppercorns**
- ☐ **2 teaspoons canned pink peppercorns**

1   Heat oil in a skillet. Cook schnitzels for 2-3 minutes on each side. Remove to serving platter and keep warm.

2   Combine skim milk and port. Reduce heat and add peppercorns to the pan. Mash lightly with a fork and pour in milk mixture, stirring to lift bits from bottom of pan. Cook over medium heat for 8-10 minutes or until sauce reduces slightly and thickens.

3   Pour sauce over schnitzels and serve immediately.

239 calories per serving

Fat	*5.3 g*	*low*
Cholesterol	*139 mg*	*medium*
Fiber	*0 g*	*low*
Sodium	*141 mg*	*low*

NUTRITION TIP
Always buy lean meat from your butcher and trim off visible fat before cooking. Remove skin from chicken and turkey.

Cook casseroles and soups a day ahead and cool in the refrigerator overnight. Any fat solidifies on the surface making it easy to remove before reheating.

When using meat juices from a roast to make gravy, add a handful of ice cubes to the gravy pan before starting. You will quickly see the fat become solid, and easy to remove – you are left with clear meat juice for a most flavorsome gravy.

Spiced Apricot Chicken, Chinese Beef with Snow Peas and Veal in Two-Peppercorn Sauce

SPICY ROAST CHICKEN

Serves 6

- ☐ **2-pound chicken**
- ☐ **2 tablespoons honey**
- ☐ **2 teaspoons sesame seeds**

SPICE MIXTURE
- ☐ **2 cloves garlic**
- ☐ **1 teaspoon grated fresh ginger**
- ☐ **2 teaspoons low-salt soy sauce**
- ☐ **3 teaspoons curry powder**
- ☐ **$\frac{1}{2}$ teaspoon garam masala**
- ☐ **3 tablespoons lemon juice**

1　Remove skin and fat from chicken and place on a roasting rack in a baking dish. To make spice mixture, blend together garlic, ginger, soy sauce, curry powder, garam masala and lemon juice; rub all over chicken. Bake at 350° for 45 minutes.
2　Warm honey and brush over chicken. Cook 15 minutes longer. Sprinkle chicken with sesame seeds 5 minutes before cooking is completed.

Pork Satays with Peanut Sauce

PORK SATAYS WITH PEANUT SAUCE

Serves 4

- ☐ **1 pound lean pork, cubed**

MARINADE
- ☐ **2 tablespoons low-salt soy sauce**
- ☐ **2 tablespoons lemon juice**
- ☐ **1 tablespoon brown sugar**
- ☐ **2 cloves garlic, crushed**
- ☐ **$\frac{1}{2}$ teaspoon ground coriander**
- ☐ **$\frac{1}{4}$ teaspoon ground cumin**
- ☐ **$\frac{1}{2}$ teaspoon grated fresh ginger**
- ☐ **freshly ground black pepper**

PEANUT SAUCE
- ☐ **1 tablespoon polyunsaturated oil**
- ☐ **1 onion, finely chopped**
- ☐ **2 cloves garlic, crushed**
- ☐ **$1\frac{1}{2}$ teaspoons curry powder**
- ☐ **3 tablespoons crunchy peanut butter**
- ☐ **2 teaspoons low-salt soy sauce**
- ☐ **$1\frac{1}{2}$ teaspoons chili sauce**
- ☐ **1 cup water**
- ☐ **2 tablespoons lemon juice**

1　To make marinade, combine soy, lemon juice, sugar, garlic, coriander, cumin and ginger in a large glass bowl. Season to taste with pepper. Add meat and marinate for 30 minutes.
2　To make sauce, heat oil in a saucepan and cook onion and garlic for 1 minute. Stir in curry powder, peanut butter, soy, chili sauce, water and lemon juice. Bring to boiling, then reduce heat and simmer, uncovered, for 5 minutes, or until sauce thickens. Set aside.
3　Remove meat from marinade and thread onto eight bamboo skewers; reserve marinade. Broil under medium heat for 8-10 minutes, turning and basting frequently with marinade. Serve satays accompanied by peanut sauce.

287 calories per serving

Fat	13.3 g	medium
Cholesterol	111 mg	medium
Fiber	2.2 g	medium
Sodium	505 mg	high

NUTRITION TIP

Marinating is an excellent way to ensure tenderness and add new flavor to meat. And it has the added bonus of keeping very lean meats juicy and tender. Try various combinations of aromatic spices and herbs with wine or low-salt soy sauce – garlic, ginger, bay leaves, lemon rind, mustard, chili, rosemary and five-star spice are all excellent.

499 calories per serving		
Fat	21.0 g	high
Cholesterol	320 mg	high
Fiber	0.2 g	low
Sodium	259 mg	low

MICROWAVE IT

Prepare chicken and rub with spice mixture as described above. Arrange chicken, breast side down, in a microwave-safe dish. Cook on HIGH (100%) for 15 minutes each side. Heat honey in a small microwave-safe dish on HIGH (100%) for 30 seconds and pour over chicken. Sprinkle with sesame seeds and cook on HIGH (100%) for 2 minutes. Stand, covered with foil, for 10 minutes before serving.

Right: High-Fiber Meat Loaf
Below: Spicy Roast Chicken

HIGH FIBER MEAT LOAF

Serves 4

- [ ] **1 pound lean ground beef**
- [ ] **$^1/_2$ cup rolled oats**
- [ ] **1 onion, grated**
- [ ] **1 medium zucchini, grated**
- [ ] **$^1/_2$ cup sultanas**
- [ ] **3 tablespoons evaporated skim milk**
- [ ] **1 egg, lightly beaten**
- [ ] **2 teaspoons grated lemon rind**
- [ ] **1 tablespoon lemon juice**
- [ ] **1 tablespoon finely chopped fresh parsley**
- [ ] **$^1/_2$ teaspoon mixed Italian herbs**
- [ ] **freshly ground black pepper**

1   Combine beef, oats, onion, zucchini, sultanas, milk, egg, lemon rind, lemon juice, parsley, herbs and pepper.
2   Press mixture into an ovenproof 9 x 5-inch loaf pan and bake at 350° for 35-40 minutes. Drain off any liquid and stand for 5 minutes before serving.

378 calories per serving		
Fat	15.0 g	medium
Cholesterol	149 mg	medium
Fiber	3.2 g	high
Sodium	138 mg	low

15

NUTRITION TIP
Try adding low-fat plain yogurt to meat recipes which list sour cream at the end (such as beef stroganoff and veal goulash), but remember not to boil after adding or it will curdle.

❖ VEAL GOULASH

Serves 4

- ☐ **4 x 1-inch thick lean veal steaks, each about ¹/₄ pound**
- ☐ **1¹/₂ tablespoons paprika**
- ☐ **2 tablespoons all-purpose flour**
- ☐ **freshly ground black pepper**
- ☐ **2 teaspoons polyunsaturated oil**
- ☐ **2 onions, chopped**
- ☐ **1 clove garlic, crushed**
- ☐ **1 tablespoon tomato paste**
- ☐ **3 tablespoons dry red wine**
- ☐ **¹/₂ cup beef stock**
- ☐ **3 tablespoons low-fat plain yogurt**
- ☐ **1 tablespoon finely chopped fresh parsley for garnish**

1   Trim meat of all visible fat and cut into 1-inch pieces. Place paprika, flour and pepper in a freezer bag; add meat and shake to coat meat evenly. Shake off excess flour mixture.

2   Heat oil in a large saucepan and cook onion and garlic for 2-3 minutes, or until onion softens. Combine tomato paste, wine and stock. Add to onion mixture with meat. Bring to boiling, then reduce heat and simmer, covered, for 20-25 minutes, or until meat is tender.

3   Remove pan from heat and stir in yogurt. Serve sprinkled with parsley.

204 calories per serving

Fat	3.7 g	low
Cholesterol	104 mg	medium
Fiber	1.0 g	low
Sodium	158 mg	low

❖ BEEF CURRY

Serves 6

- ☐ **2 pounds lean topside steak**
- ☐ **2 onions, chopped**
- ☐ **1 clove garlic, crushed**
- ☐ **1 teaspoon grated fresh ginger**
- ☐ **1 tablespoon dry white wine**
- ☐ **2 teaspoons low-salt soy sauce**
- ☐ **¹/₄ teaspoon curry paste (vindaloo)**
- ☐ **2 teaspoons curry powder**
- ☐ **¹/₂ teaspoon ground turmeric**
- ☐ **¹/₂ teaspoon ground cumin**
- ☐ **3 cardamom pods**
- ☐ **2 tablespoons mango chutney**
- ☐ **1 cup beef stock**
- ☐ **2 teaspoons cornstarch blended with 2 tablespoons water**

1   Trim meat of all visible fat and cut into 1-inch cubes. Combine meat, onions, garlic, ginger, wine, soy, curry paste, curry powder, turmeric, cumin, cardamom, chutney and stock in a saucepan.

Above: Spicy Marinated Lamb Kebabs
Left: Veal Goulash and Beef Curry

2   Bring curry mixture to boiling, then reduce heat and simmer, covered, for 1¹/₄ hours or until steak is tender.

3   Remove cover and continue to cook 15 minutes longer. Whisk in cornstarch mixture and cook until curry boils and thickens.

336 calories per serving

Fat	5.8 g	low
Cholesterol	168 mg	medium
Fiber	1.1 g	low
Sodium	277 mg	low

❖ SPICY MARINATED LAMB KEBABS

Serves 4

- ☐ **1 pound lean lamb, cubed**
- ☐ **1 large green pepper, cubed**
- ☐ **16 button mushrooms**
- ☐ **2 medium zucchini, sliced into 1-inch pieces**

MARINADE

- ☐ **2 tablespoons honey**
- ☐ **1 tablespoon low-salt soy sauce**
- ☐ **1 clove garlic, crushed**
- ☐ **¹/₂ teaspoon ground cinnamon**
- ☐ **2 teaspoons sesame oil**

1   To make marinade, combine honey, soy, garlic, cinnamon and sesame oil in a glass bowl. Add meat and marinate for 30 minutes.

2   Remove meat from marinade and thread meat onto eight bamboo skewers, alternating with peppers, mushrooms and zucchini. Grill over medium heat for 8-10 minutes, turning frequently and basting with marinade.

339 calories per serving

Fat	12.2 g	medium
Cholesterol	136 mg	medium
Fiber	2.6 g	medium
Sodium	244 mg	low

STIR-FRY CHICKEN AND BROCCOLI

Serves 4

- ☐ 2 tablespoons polyunsaturated oil
- ☐ 2 onions, cut into eighths
- ☐ 1 clove garlic, crushed
- ☐ 1 teaspoon grated fresh ginger
- ☐ 8 boned chicken breasts, cut into thin strips
- ☐ 1 broccoli head (about $1/2$ pound), cut into flowerets
- ☐ $1/4$ teaspoon ground cumin
- ☐ $1/4$ teaspoon ground coriander
- ☐ 3 tablespoons oyster sauce
- ☐ 1 teaspoon sesame oil
- ☐ 1 tablespoon sesame seeds

1   Heat oil in a skillet or wok. Stir-fry onions, garlic and ginger for 2-3 minutes, or until onion softens. Remove from pan and set aside.

2   Combine cumin, coriander, oyster sauce and sesame oil. Add chicken to the pan and stir-fry for 3-4 minutes. Return onion mixture to the pan; add broccoli and spices mixture. Stir-fry for 2-3 minutes or until broccoli is just tender. Serve sprinkled with sesame seeds.

356 calories per serving

Fat	*20.8 g*	*medium*
Cholesterol	*120 mg*	*medium*
Fiber	*2.9 g*	*medium*
Sodium	*787 mg*	*high*

MARINATED BEEF KEBABS

Serves 4

- ☐ 1 pound lean topside steak
- ☐ 8 small onions, peeled
- ☐ $1/4$ pound button mushrooms
- ☐ $1/2$ red pepper, cubed
- ☐ $1/2$ green pepper, cubed

MARINADE

- ☐ $3/4$ cup low-fat plain yogurt
- ☐ 2 teaspoons wholegrain mustard
- ☐ 1 tablespoon finely chopped gherkin pickle
- ☐ 1 clove garlic, crushed
- ☐ 2 tablespoons dry sherry
- ☐ freshly ground black pepper

1   Trim all visible fat from meat and cut into 1-inch cubes. Combine yogurt, mustard, gherkin, garlic, sherry and pepper in a glass bowl. Add meat and marinate for 1 hour.

2   Remove meat from marinade and thread meat onto eight bamboo skewers, alternating with onions, mushrooms and peppers. Grill kebabs over medium heat for 8-10 minutes, turning and basting frequently with marinade. Serve kebabs with any remaining marinade as an accompaniment.

488 calories per serving

Fat	*31.9 g*	*high*
Cholesterol	*109 mg*	*medium*
Fiber	*5.8 g*	*high*
Sodium	*403 mg*	*medium*

CHICKEN AND LIMA BEAN BAKE

Serves 6

- ☐ 1 slice bacon, chopped
- ☐ 2-pound chicken, skinned
- ☐ 2 onions, chopped
- ☐ 1 clove garlic, crushed
- ☐ $1/2$ cup chicken stock
- ☐ 4 tablespoons white wine
- ☐ 1 teaspoon mixed Italian herbs
- ☐ 1 teaspoon sugar
- ☐ 15-ounce can peeled tomatoes, undrained and mashed
- ☐ 10-ounce can lima beans, drained

1   Place bacon in a skillet and cook for 2-3 minutes, or until crisp. Remove from pan and set aside. Brown chicken pieces in bacon drippings; remove from pan. Add onion and garlic and cook for 2-3 minutes, until onion softens. Transfer chicken and onion mixture to an ovenproof dish.

2   Add stock, wine, herbs, sugar and tomatoes to pan and cook over medium heat until mixture boils and thickens, stirring occasionally. Add lima beans. Sprinkle chicken with bacon and pour sauce over. Cover and bake at 400° for 1 hour, or until chicken is tender.

103 calories per serving

Fat	*2.8 g*	*low*
Cholesterol	*7 mg*	*low*
Fiber	*2.7 g*	*medium*
Sodium	*333 mg*	*medium*

Stir-fry Chicken and Broccoli, and Marinated Beef Kebabs

Chicken and Lima Bean Bake

CLASSIC LIGHT

BEEF AND MUSHROOM PIE

Serves 6

- ☐ **1 pound lean topside steak**
- ☐ **4 tablespoons polyunsaturated oil**
- ☐ **1 onion, chopped**
- ☐ **$1/_4$ pound mushrooms, sliced**
- ☐ **$1^1/_4$ cups beef stock**
- ☐ **freshly ground black pepper**
- ☐ **2 tablespoons cornstarch blended with 4 tablespoons water**
- ☐ **12 sheets filo pastry**
- ☐ **1 tablespoon poppy seeds**

1   Trim meat of all visible fat and cut into 1-inch cubes. Heat 1 tablespoon oil in a large saucepan and cook onion and mushrooms for 2-3 minutes.

2   Add meat and stock to pan. Season to taste with pepper. Bring to boiling, then reduce heat and simmer for $1^1/_2$-2 hours, or until meat is tender. Remove cover and return to boiling. Whisk in cornstarch mixture, stirring until sauce thickens. Cool.

3   Layer pastry sheets on top of each other, brushing between layers with remaining oil. Place a 9-inch pie plate upside down on pastry and cut a circle 1-inch larger than dish through all the layers of pastry.

4   Line pie plate with eight cut pastry layers. Spread filling over pastry and top with remaining four pastry layers. Roll down edges of pastry and brush top with oil. Sprinkle with poppy seeds. Bake at 350° for 30 minutes, or until golden brown.

214 calories per serving

Fat	*14.6 g*	*medium*
Cholesterol	*53 mg*	*low*
Fiber	*1.3 g*	*low*
Sodium	*316 mg*	*medium*

HOW WE'VE CUT FAT AND CALORIES

✧ Instead of the traditional shortcrust or puff pastry, we have used sheets of fine filo pastry which have been brushed sparingly with oil. Not only is the fat content reduced, but the pastry is crisp and light, never soggy.

✧ Lean beef has been selected for the filling and cooked with vegetables for extra flavor and fiber. The pie ends up being modest in fat, salt and calories – a satisfying, yet healthy, pie that everyone can enjoy.

GETTING
STARTED

*Try the following 7-day Menu Planner to help you on the road
to a slimmer, healthier body. Based on our low-fat recipes, each
day offers suggestions for breakfast, lunch and dinner.*

This plan is suitable for moderately active women and should allow a weight loss of 1 to 2 pounds a week. Any more than this is usually fluid and will be regained once the diet is finished. Men should aim for 1800 calories by including two more slices of bread, a piece of fruit or a vegetable.

Our 7-day Plan aims to help you understand and prepare a balanced nutritious food plan. It's a good idea to try each day's meals for variety, but you can swap meals or make substitutes, depending on your lifestyle, your food preferences and availability ($1/_2$ cup cooked rice, for example, is equivalent to one medium potato or one slice of bread or $1/_2$ cup cooked pasta).

Each day: 1 cup whole milk or $1 1/_2$ cups low-fat milk or 2 cups skim milk for tea, coffee, or cereal. For spreading and cooking, use 1 tablespoon butter or oil.

USING OUR ANALYSIS

Each recipe has been analyzed for its content of calories, fat, cholesterol, dietary fiber and sodium (an indication of salt) for each serving. At a glance, you can see whether each dish is low, medium or high in each nutrient.

Most of the recipes are LOW in fat, cholesterol and sodium and MEDIUM or HIGH in fiber. But occasionally if you find one that is HIGH in fat or sodium, balance out the remainder of your meals with less fat and salt. Similarly if your day's recipes are LOW in fiber, add some extra in the form of vegetables, salad, wholegrain bread or whole fruit.

A recipe analyzed as HIGH in calories or fat does not mean it is too fattening a dish. Rather, it lets you know that on a diet intake it ranks higher than others.

DAILY GUIDE

Calories (acceptable diet level)
1200–1500   Women
1500–1800   Men

Fat (based on 30% of calories)
50 g

Cholesterol
300 mg

Fiber
25–30 g

Sodium
920–2300 mg

PANTRY PLANNER

Check this easy pantry planner before you go shopping to ensure that you get the special items you need for your Be Healthy Be Slim diet.

STAPLE ITEMS
bran, bread, bread crumbs (dried), filo pastry, dried fruits, dried herbs and spices, gelatin, nuts, pasta, rice (white and brown), rolled oats
CANNED FOODS
beans, evaporated skim milk, fruit in natural juice, salmon, tomatoes (whole peeled), tuna
DAIRY PRODUCTS
polyunsaturated margarine, cheese, cottage/ricotta cheese, eggs, low-fat milk, plain low-fat yogurt
SAUCES AND MUSTARDS
chili sauce, selection of mustards, low-salt soy sauce, red pepper seasoning, tomato sauce, Worcestershire sauce
VINEGARS AND OILS
olive oil, polyunsaturated oils, sesame oil, vinegar (white, brown, cider)
FRESH PRODUCE
fruit, vegetables and herbs

NUTRITION HINTS

SHOPPING
Never shop when you're hungry – studies show that hunger triggers more food purchases than originally planned.

Always shop from a list. This avoids impulse buys and "supermarket specials" of high-calorie items that you may be tempted to eat later.

Try to buy fresh produce at a top-quality fruit and vegetable market. Seeing lots of attractive fruit and crisp vegetables at the peak of their ripeness is the best way to tempt yourself (and the family) into enjoying more of them.

Walk past cake shops, chocolate shops and patisseries without looking in the window. It's true – out of sight is out of mind!

KITCHEN
Keep food out of sight – store food in containers, in cupboards and at the back of the fridge.

Don't leave chocolates, sweets, nuts or fruit around the house. Often the mere sight of food will trigger a desire to eat (not true hunger). Make it easy for yourself by not having to confront food all the time.

Try not to keep unhealthy foods in the kitchen or ask other members of the family to help themselves.

❖
DAY 1

Breakfast
$1/_2$ grapefruit or $1/_2$ orange
Untoasted muesli with low-fat milk
Wholewheat toast, spread thinly with
butter or margarine
Tea, coffee or low-fat milk

Lunch
Lasagna (p.37)
Italian Green Bean Salad (p.49)
or tossed green salad
Fresh mango
or fresh pineapple slice
Mineral water
or sugar free soft drink

Dinner
Lemon Fish Parcels (p.7)
Pumpkin Soufflé (p.50)
or mashed potato
Broccoli or cauliflower
Blueberry and Apple Crunch (p.60)

❖
DAY 2

Breakfast
Banana smoothie shake: 1 cup low-fat
milk, 1 banana, honey and vanilla extract
combined until smooth in a blender

Lunch
Open sandwich – Tomato and Cucumber
on Rye (p.28) or salad sandwich on
wholewheat bread
Carton low-fat natural yogurt with fresh
strawberries

Dinner
Stir-fry Noodles with Pork and
Vegetables (p.35)
Wedge of Baked Cheesecake (p.64) or
scoop vanilla ice cream

BY MEAL
PLANNER

Breakfast
Lunch
Dinner

❖
DAY 3

Breakfast
Orange juice
Egg, boiled or poached
Wholewheat toast, spread thinly with
butter or margarine
Tea, coffee or low-fat milk

Lunch
Marinated Fish Salad (p.4)
or 3-ounce can tuna or salmon, drained,
with mixed salad
Crusty mixed grain bread roll
Wedge of cheese with water biscuits

Dinner
Orange Chicken (p.16)
Baked potato
Zucchini or Brussels sprouts
Serving of Grapefruit and Pineapple
Sorbet (p.62)
or carton low-fat fruit yogurt

❖
DAY 4

Breakfast
Wedge of cantaloupe
Wholewheat or bran cereal with low-fat
milk

Crumpet or toast, spread lightly with
butter or margarine
Tea, coffee or low-fat milk

Lunch
Fresh Vegetable Salad with
Peanut Sauce (p.34)
Wedge of Hazelnut Torte (p.60)
or sugar-free jelly and ice cream

Dinner
Chinese Beef with Snow Peas (p.12)
Steamed rice
Chinese Sesame Slaw (p.46)
Serving of Summer's Day Freeze (p.58)
or fruit salad

❖
DAY 5

Breakfast
Rolled oats with low-fat milk
Wholewheat toast, spread thinly with
butter or margarine plus cottage cheese
and tomato slices

Lunch
Chicken and Corn Soup (p.31)
Crispbread or wholewheat bread
Wedge of Spicy Apple Cake (p.60) or
handful of raisins, sultanas and dried
apricots

Dinner
Veal Goulash (p.19)
Boiled noodles
Broccoli or string beans
Oranges in Liqueur with Cinnamon-
Yogurt Sauce (p.62)
or Lemon and Passionfruit Cream (p.58)

❖
DAY 6

Breakfast
Tomato juice
Small can baked beans, heated and served
on a toasted muffin half
Tea, coffee or low-fat milk

Lunch
Best-ever Hamburgers (p.34)
Fresh peach or pear

Dinner
Pasta with Herb Sauce (p.28)
Tossed green salad
Strawberries and Kiwifruit in Wine (p.62)
or fresh strawberries or raspberries

❖
DAY 7

Breakfast
Bran cereal with ¹/₂ sliced banana and
low-fat milk
Fresh roll or crusty bread spread with
cottage cheese or peanut butter

Lunch
Grilled cheese and tomato on wholewheat
toast
Small bunch grapes or cherries

Dinner
Chilled Curry Chicken Salad (p.34)
Rice or potato salad
Spiced Prune and Apricot Compote
(p.63)

EATING OUT

With the popularity of lighter, fresher cooking, it is now possible to eat out, eat healthily and enjoy it.

Best choices for starters are fresh oysters, smoked salmon, clear broth, warm salad, melon and ham, seafood salad or grilled foods (avoid deep-fried). Stick to lean meats, fish, seafood, veal, chicken, beef or pork cooked without rich sauces or pastry. Ask for extra vegetables or choose vegetables plus salad. Order two entrées in place of an entrée and main course. Suggested desserts are based on fruit – so light and refreshing after a big meal. Strawberries, mango, cantaloupe or fruit salad are almost always on the menu or can be prepared in minutes by the chef.

WHEN ORDERING

Order first so you don't change your mind upon hearing others' choices. Don't be embarrassed to ask for meat without sauce or gravy, fish grilled "dry" without butter, plain salad or extra vegetables. Split a course with a friend – ask for an extra plate or another spoon. Order water as well as wine – you'll find you're quite satisfied with one glass of wine if you can refresh yourself with a glass of water too.

SLOW EATING

Eat slowly and chew well – really enjoy the flavor of the food. Put your fork down between each mouthful. Get involved in conversation. Never face a rich meal feeling ravenous. Eat something to take the edge off your appetite before you leave home. Always eat vegetables or salad, meat or fish first. If your plate has been piled high with fattening foods, like chips, you can leave those until last – then you may even leave some uneaten. When everyone else is eating dessert, order coffee at the same time and linger over it instead.

LET'S HAVE A DRINK

Iced water, soda water, mineral water or diet drinks add no calories and are the best choices for the dieter dining out. Alcohol itself is fattening, supplying more calories gram for gram than either carbohydrate or protein. It also stimulates the appetite, so you tend to eat more. Fancy cocktails and liqueurs with their cream and fizzy drinks can really stack on the calories and are best avoided.

DRINK	QUANTITY	CALS
Beer, regular	1 can or ¹/₂ pint	130
	1 pint	210
Beer, low alcohol	1 can or ¹/₂ pint	95
	1 pint	150
Cider, dry	1 glass	70
Cider, sweet	1 glass	85
Liqueurs (Drambuie, Grand Marnier, Cointreau)	1 jigger	75
Port, muscat	1 small glass	85
Sherry	1 small glass	60
Soft drinks (cola, lemonade, ginger ale)	1 glass	65
Spirits (brandy, gin, scotch, vodka)	1 jigger	65
Stout	1 glass	75
Vermouth, dry	1 small glass	60
Vermouth, sweet	1 small glass	85
Wine, red	1 glass	70
Wine, white dry	1 glass	65
Wine, sparkling	1 glass	75
Wine, sweet dessert	1 glass	90

BEST CUISINES

BEWARE OF FAST FOOD

Fast food is generally high in fat, cholesterol and salt with little in the way of fiber – there are no filling vegetables, salads or fruit. Portion sizes are "whopper" or "super", making it easy to overconsume more calories than you imagine. Because deep-frying is quick, convenient and appealing, especially on cold days, many take-away foods are prepared this way. But it's a calorie-laden way to eat and a danger for dieters. The type of fat in fast foods is mainly saturated, the worst kind for your heart. Even if specified as "vegetable oil", this can be palm oil, a saturated tropical oil often favored by food manufacturers and processors because of its price and stability.

DO ORDER: Hamburgers with salad, Steak sandwiches, Asian and Oriental mixed dishes, Pizza, Barbecued chicken (skin removed).

BEST AVOIDED: Soft drinks, Milk shakes, Iced coffee, French fries, Potato scallops, Battered chicken pieces, Fried seafood, Fried spring rolls, Battered sausages

ITALIAN

DO ORDER: Vegetable antipasto (peppers, marinated vegetables, tomato salad, etc), Minestrone or vegetable soup, Grissini bread sticks, Crusty bread (no butter), Calamari salad, Prosciutto (smoked ham) and melon, Ravioli filled with meat or spinach, Tortellini stuffed with ricotta, Spaghetti, fettuccine or other pasta with the following sauces: Napolitana (tomato), Marinara (seafood), Bolognese (meat), Primavera (vegetables), Putanesca (tomato, vegetable and olives), or mussels, Chicken cacciatore, Grilled garlic chicken (remove skin), Veal scaloppine (no cream sauces), Osso bucco (veal shanks in lemony tomatoes), Pizza with thin crisp crust (avoid too much cheese), Gelato, Fresh fruits

BEST AVOIDED: Garlic or herb bread, Salami, Pepperoni, Fried calamari, Frittomisto (fried seafood), Cannelloni, Lasagna, Pasta with cream sauces (Carbonara, Alfredo and Bosciola), Saltimbocca (veal with ham and cheese), Zabaglione, Cassata

CHINESE

DO ORDER: Clear short soups with or without wontons or dumplings, Crab and corn soup, Steamed dim sims or wontons (avoid fried), Sang choy bow (pork and lettuce rolls), Satay shrimp, Steamed fish with black bean sauce, Combination vegetables, Stir-fry dishes with lean meat, chicken or pork, Steamed rice, Chow mein dishes, Chop suey dishes, Mongolian hot-pot, Chinese tea, Lychees

BEST AVOIDED: Deep-fried shrimp cutlets, Deep-fried entrées (spring rolls, dim sims, crab balls, and so on), Crispy-skin chicken, Chicken in lemon sauce, Sweet and sour dishes, Fried rice, Fried noodles, Peking duck, Pork spare ribs (unless lean), Deep-fried whole fish, Chicken wings

MIDDLE EASTERN

DO ORDER: Houmous (chick pea dip), Baba ghanoush (eggplant dip), Flatbread, pita bread, Tabbouleh (parsley and tomato salad), Kafta, Shish kebabs and souvlaki, Shawarma or donor kebab (spit roasted beef with salad on flatbread), Kibbi (baked meat and wheat slices), Rice-stuffed marrow or zucchini, Yogurt and cucumber dip, Foules mesdames (marinated beans)

BEST AVOIDED: Falafel (fried chick peas), Spicy sausages, Baklava, Bread with oil or melted butter

INDIAN

DO ORDER: Tandoori chicken or lean meats, Kebabs, Beef, lamb or chicken vindaloo (hot spicy curry), Vegetable curries, Dahl (spiced lentils), Naan, roti (Indian breads), Lean meat curries (avoid rich coconut sauces), Steamed rice, Fish or shrimp curry (avoid rich coconut sauces), Lamb or beef with spinach, Kashmir lamb curry, Cucumber and yogurt sambal, Chutneys (small quantities), Chicken biriani (chicken, rice and vegetables), Dosa (filled pancake)

BEST AVOIDED: Samosas, Papadams, Parathas, Puri, Chicken or beef korma (cashew sauce), Coconut sambal

LIGHT AND LEAN
SNACKS

Snacking does not have to be bad for you – our recipes for tempting light and lean snacks are loaded with fresh salad, herbs, vegetables and lots more for tasty snacks at any time.

PASTA WITH HERB SAUCE

This tasty low calorie sauce is also great poured over steamed vegetables. You can use it as an original alternative to white sauce.

Serves 4

- [ ] **1 pound mixed colored spiral pasta**
- [ ] **fresh herbs for garnish (optional)**

HERB SAUCE
- [ ] **1 tablespoon polyunsaturated margarine**
- [ ] **1 small onion, chopped**
- [ ] **1 clove garlic, crushed**
- [ ] **2 tablespoons all-purpose flour**
- [ ] **1/2 cup vegetable stock**
- [ ] **1 cup low-fat plain yogurt**
- [ ] **2 tablespoons finely chopped fresh parsley**
- [ ] **2 tablespoons finely chopped fresh basil**
- [ ] **2 tablespoons finely chopped fresh chives**
- [ ] **freshly ground black pepper**

1   Cook pasta according to package directions. Drain and keep warm.
2   To make sauce, melt margarine in a saucepan and cook onion and garlic for 2-3 minutes. Stir in flour and stock and continue to cook until sauce thickens.
3   Stir in yogurt and heat gently. Mix in parsley, basil and chives. Season with pepper. Spoon sauce over pasta and serve garnished with additional fresh herbs if you wish.

231 calories per serving

Fat	4.6 g	low
Cholesterol	4 mg	low
Fiber	2.2 g	medium
Sodium	133 mg	low

MICROWAVE IT
While the pasta is cooking on the stovetop, you can make the sauce in your microwave oven. Place margarine, onion and garlic in a microwave-safe jug; cook on HIGH (100%) for 2 minutes. Stir in flour and stock. Cook on HIGH (100%) for 2 minutes, until sauce thickens. Add yogurt; cook on MEDIUM (50%) for 2 minutes, until just heated through. Mix in herbs and season with pepper.

WARM SEAFOOD SALAD

Our warm seafood salad makes a marvelous light meal in spring or autumn when there is a slight chill in the air.

Serves 6

- [ ] **1/2 bunch watercress**
- [ ] **mignonette lettuce leaves**
- [ ] **butter lettuce leaves**
- [ ] **1 tablespoon olive oil**
- [ ] **1 onion, thinly sliced**
- [ ] **1 clove garlic, crushed**
- [ ] **1/2 pound scallops, cleaned**
- [ ] **1/2 pound shrimp, shelled and deveined**
- [ ] **1/2 pound firm white fish fillets**
- [ ] **freshly ground black pepper**
- [ ] **fresh dill sprigs for garnish**

DRESSING
- [ ] **1/2 cup lime juice**
- [ ] **1 tablespoon olive oil**
- [ ] **freshly ground black pepper**
- [ ] **1 tablespoon finely chopped fresh dill**

1   Arrange watercress and lettuce leaves on individual dinner plates.
2   In a non-stick skillet, heat oil and cook onion and garlic until soft. Add scallops, shrimp and fish and cook for 5-6 minutes or until shrimp turn pink and fish is just cooked. Season with pepper. Arrange fish mixture over lettuce leaves.

3   To make dressing, combine lime juice, oil, pepper and dill in a screwtop jar and shake well to combine. Sprinkle over fish, garnish with dill sprigs and serve immediately.

189 calories per serving

Fat	8.0 g	low
Cholesterol	112 mg	medium
Fiber	1.6 g	medium
Sodium	340 mg	medium

TOMATO AND CUCUMBER ON RYE

Our sophisticated version of a salad sandwich with its tangy vinaigrette dressing is cool and refreshing in the summer heat.

Makes 4 sandwiches

- [ ] **2 medium tomatoes, thinly sliced**
- [ ] **1/2 cucumber, thinly sliced**
- [ ] **1/2 green pepper, diced**
- [ ] **3 green onions, thinly sliced**
- [ ] **1 stalk celery, chopped**
- [ ] **1/2 bunch watercress**
- [ ] **4 slices rye bread**

DRESSING
- [ ] **3 tablespoons white wine vinegar**
- [ ] **1 tablespoon olive oil**
- [ ] **1/2 teaspoon mustard powder**
- [ ] **pinch chili powder**
- [ ] **freshly ground black pepper**

1   In a bowl combine tomatoes, cucumber, pepper, green onions and celery.
2   To make dressing, combine vinegar, oil, mustard, chili and pepper in a screw top jar. Shake well to combine and pour over tomato salad.
3   Divide watercress between bread slices, and top with tomato salad.

142 calories per serving

Fat	5.0 g	low
Cholesterol	0 mg	low
Fiber	5.2 g	high
Sodium	192 mg	low

Pasta with Herb Sauce, Warm Seafood Salad and Tomato and Cucumber on Rye

CURRIED PUMPKIN SOUP

You'll find this soup not only easy but delicious and healthy as a main course for a winter luncheon. Try serving it with herb croutons followed by a fresh salad.

Serves 4

- ☐ **1 tablespoon polyunsaturated oil**
- ☐ **1 large onion, chopped**
- ☐ **$^1/_2$ teaspoon ground coriander**
- ☐ **$^1/_2$ teaspoon ground cumin**
- ☐ **$^1/_2$ teaspoon chili powder**
- ☐ **3 cups canned pumpkin**
- ☐ **4 cups chicken stock**
- ☐ **freshly ground black pepper**

1   Heat oil in a large saucepan. Cook onion, coriander, cumin and chili powder until onion softens.
2   Stir pumpkin into saucepan with stock. Cook pumpkin for 20 minutes or until tender, then cool slightly. Transfer soup in batches to a food processor or blender and process until smooth.
3   Return soup to a rinsed saucepan and heat. Season to taste with pepper.

144 calories per serving

Fat	3.4 g	low
Cholesterol	0 mg	low
Fiber	1.9 g	medium
Sodium	193 mg	low

Minted Green Pea Soup and Curried Pumpkin Soup

MINTED GREEN PEA SOUP

This soup evokes summer. Use fresh peas, otherwise use frozen peas, as we have. Add a swirl of yogurt and a sprig of mint to make this an elegant dish.

Serves 6

- ☐ **4 cups chicken stock**
- ☐ **1 onion, chopped**
- ☐ **1 tablespoon polyunsaturated oil**
- ☐ **1 large potato, diced**
- ☐ **$^1/_2$ lettuce, shredded**
- ☐ **1 pound frozen peas**
- ☐ **1 tablespoon chopped fresh mint**
- ☐ **freshly ground black pepper**
- ☐ **6 tablespoons low-fat plain yogurt**
- ☐ **fresh mint sprigs for garnish**

1   Heat oil in a saucepan. Cook onion for 2-3 minutes, or until soft. Add stock, potato, lettuce, peas and mint , and simmer for 20 minutes, or until potato is tender. Season with pepper. Set aside to cool.
2   Transfer soup mixture in batches to the bowl of a food processor or blender. Process until smooth. Chill for at least 2 hours before serving.
3   To serve, garnish with a tablespoon of yogurt, swirled through each bowl of soup, and a sprig of mint.

115 calories per serving

Fat	2.2 g	low
Cholesterol	1 mg	low
Fiber	7.2 g	high
Sodium	155 mg	low

COOK'S TIP

If you plan to serve this soup and the day dawns cold and rainy, there is no need to worry. It is equally delicious served hot, accompanied with hot croutons.

Chilled Tomato and Zucchini Soup and Chicken with Corn Soup

HERB CROUTONS

- ☐ **4 slices multiwheat bread**
- ☐ **2 tablespoons olive oil**
- ☐ **1 tablespoon chopped fresh parsley**
- ☐ **1 tablespoon chopped fresh thyme**
- ☐ **1 tablespoon snipped fresh chives**
- ☐ **1 tablespoon sesame seeds**
- ☐ **freshly ground black pepper**

1   Cut crusts from bread and brush very lightly with oil.
2   Combine parsley, thyme, chives and sesame seeds. Season with pepper.
3   Sprinkle a tablespoon of mixture over each bread slice. Cut each slice into cubes, place on a cookie sheet and bake at 400° for 10-15 minutes, or until croutons are golden and crisp. Serve hot with soup.

165 calories per serving

Fat	10.5 g	medium
Cholesterol	0 mg	low
Fiber	1.7 g	medium
Sodium	149 mg	low

COOK'S TIP
Croutons are often thought of as high in fat and therefore not included in weight watchers' diets. These croutons will, however, allow you to indulge and are the perfect accompaniment to many soups. This recipe is enough for four people.

❖ CHILLED TOMATO AND ZUCCHINI SOUP

Start any dinner party with this easy-to-make refreshing summer soup – and no one will guess just how few calories there are in it! Our tomato-mint ice cubes add that special touch but plain ice cubes work just as well.

Serves 4

- ☐ **1 tablespoon olive oil**
- ☐ **1 onion, chopped**
- ☐ **1 clove garlic, crushed**
- ☐ **4 cups vegetable stock**
- ☐ **4 tablespoons finely chopped fresh mint**
- ☐ **15-ounce can peeled tomatoes**
- ☐ **2 zucchini, coarsely grated**
- ☐ **freshly ground black pepper**

Spicy Rice Tomatoes and Vegetables (recipe page 32)

TOMATO-MINT ICE CUBES
- ☐ **fresh mint leaves**
- ☐ **³/₄ cup tomato juice**
- ☐ **³/₄ cup water**

1   Heat oil in a large saucepan. Cook onion and garlic for 2-3 minutes, or until onion softens. Add stock and mint, and simmer for 5 minutes. Set aside to cool.
2   Place tomatoes and stock mixture in a food processor or blender and process until soup is smooth. Stir in zucchini and season with pepper. Refrigerate until well chilled.
3   To make tomato-mint ice cubes, place a mint leaf in each space of an ice cube tray. Mix together tomato juice and water, and pour into the ice cube tray. Freeze. To serve, place ice cubes in each soup bowl and pour chilled soup over.

78 calories per serving

Fat	4.3 g	low
Cholesterol	0 mg	low
Fiber	2.8 g	high
Sodium	389 mg	medium

❖ CHICKEN AND CORN SOUP

If you add puréed vegetables to thicken this hearty dish, you will not need calorie-filled thickeners and your soup will be delicious and full of goodness.

Serves 6

- ☐ **1 large potato, diced**
- ☐ **1 large onion, sliced**
- ☐ **6 cups chicken stock**
- ☐ **¹/₂ teaspoon chili powder, or according to taste**
- ☐ **1 cup chopped cooked chicken**
- ☐ **12-ounce can whole kernel corn**
- ☐ **2 tablespoons finely chopped fresh parsley**
- ☐ **freshly ground black pepper**

1   Place potato, onion, stock and chili powder in a large saucepan and simmer for 20 minutes, or until vegetables are tender.
2   Remove vegetables using a slotted spoon and purée in a food processor or blender. Return to stock mixture and whisk to combine. Stir in chicken and corn, and heat gently for about 10 minutes. Add parsley and season to taste with pepper.

197 calories per serving

Fat	4.5 g	low
Cholesterol	53 mg	low
Fiber	4.1 g	high
Sodium	222 mg	low

COOK'S TIP
Use this method of thickening soup for any soup containing vegetables such as potatoes, pumpkin or sweet potatoes.

roughly chopped
- ☐ ¹/₂ cup dry white wine
- ☐ 1 tablespoon finely chopped fresh basil
- ☐ ¹/₂ teaspoon dried thyme
- ☐ ¹/₂ teaspoon dried oregano
- ☐ freshly ground black pepper
- ☐ Parmesan cheese, for serving

1   Cook pasta according to package directions. Drain and keep warm.
2   To make sauce, place eggplant, onion, garlic, pepper, zucchini, tomatoes, wine, basil, thyme, oregano and pepper in a non-stick skillet. Cook over low heat for 30-45 minutes, stirring occasionally.
3   Spoon sauce over pasta and serve sprinkled with a little Parmesan cheese.

523 calories per serving

Fat	*6.3 g*	*low*
Cholesterol	*9 mg*	*low*
Fiber	*19 g*	*high*
Sodium	*150 mg*	*low*

❖

FETTUCCINE WITH SPICY SEAFOOD SAUCE

Accompany this simple spicy meal with a salad made of your favorite vegetables. Try combining raw spinach, orange segments, thinly sliced mushrooms and shallots, tossed in a tasty low-calorie dressing.

Serves 4

- ☐ 1 pound mixed colored fettuccine

SPICY SEAFOOD SAUCE
- ☐ 1 tablespoon olive oil
- ☐ 1 onion, sliced
- ☐ 1 red pepper, diced
- ☐ 1 clove garlic, crushed
- ☐ 1 red chili, seeded and finely chopped
- ☐ ¹/₂ teaspoon ground cumin
- ☐ ¹/₂ teaspoon ground coriander
- ☐ 15-ounce can peeled tomatoes, undrained and mashed
- ☐ 3 tablespoons dry white wine
- ☐ 1 tablespoon tomato paste
- ☐ ¹/₄ pound calamari, sliced into rings
- ☐ ¹/₄ pound cleaned fresh mussels in shells
- ☐ 1 pound shrimp, peeled and deveined
- ☐ 4 tablespoons finely chopped fresh coriander

1   Cook pasta according to package directions. Drain and keep warm.
2   To make sauce, heat oil in a saucepan. Cook onion, pepper, garlic, chili, cumin and coriander until onion softens. Add

---

SPICY RICE, TOMATOES AND VEGETABLES

Serving steamed snow peas with this wonderfully colored rice and vegetable dish to make an attractive light meal. Alternatively, try it as a side dish to serve six. It is particularly good with grilled chicken.

Serves 4

- ☐ 1 tablespoon olive oil
- ☐ 1 onion, sliced
- ☐ 1 green pepper, diced
- ☐ 1 red chili, seeded and finely chopped
- ☐ ³/₄ cup white rice
- ☐ ³/₄ cup quick-cooking brown rice
- ☐ 15-ounce can peeled tomatoes, undrained and roughly chopped
- ☐ 1¹/₂ cups vegetable stock or water
- ☐ freshly ground black pepper

1   Heat oil in a large saucepan. Cook onion, pepper and chili for 3-4 minutes. Add rice, mix well and cook for 3-4 minutes.
2   Add tomatoes to the pan with stock or water. Bring to the boil and simmer for 30 minutes, or until liquid is absorbed and rice is tender. Season with pepper.

182 calories per serving

Fat	*4.6 g*	*low*
Cholesterol	*0 mg*	*low*
Fiber	*2.3 g*	*high*
Sodium	*36 mg*	*low*

Spaghetti with Ratatouille Sauce, Fettuccine with Spicy Seafood Sauce and Ricotta and Tuna Cannelloni

MICROWAVE IT

This dish is easily cooked in the microwave oven. In a large microwave-safe jug cook onion, pepper and chili in oil for 2 minutes. Add rice and cook 1 minute longer. Mix in tomatoes and stock or water. Season with pepper. Cook, uncovered, on HIGH (100%) for 15-20 minutes, or until all the liquid is absorbed and the rice is tender.

❖

SPAGHETTI WITH RATATOUILLE SAUCE

Use this delicious and versatile ratatouille sauce as a topping for baked potatoes or eat it on its own, hot or cold. The length of cooking time depends upon whether you wish the texture to be crunchy or very soft.

Serves 4

- ☐ 1 pound wholewheat spaghetti

RATATOUILLE
- ☐ 1 medium eggplant, diced
- ☐ 1 large onion, sliced
- ☐ 1 clove garlic, crushed
- ☐ 1 green pepper, diced
- ☐ 2 zucchini, diced
- ☐ 1 pound tomatoes, peeled and

tomatoes, wine and tomato paste. Cook over medium heat for 30 minutes longer, or until sauce reduces and thickens. Add calamari and cook for 5 minutes or until just tender. Add mussels and shrimp and cook for 4-5 minutes. Mix in 2 tablespoons coriander. Pour sauce over pasta and serve garnished with remaining coriander.

426 calories per serving

Fat	8.7 g	low
Cholesterol	325 mg	high
Fiber	3.5 g	high
Sodium	710 mg	high

❖

RICOTTA AND TUNA CANNELLONI

Rather than making up the cannelloni from lasagna sheets, as we have done, you may prefer to use bought cannelloni tubes.

Serves 4

- ☐ **2 sheets fresh tomato lasagna**
- ☐ **4 tablespoons grated Parmesan cheese**
- ☐ **fresh dill for garnish**

FILLING
- ☐ **1 onion, finely sliced**
- ☐ **1 clove garlic, crushed**
- ☐ **¼ pound mushrooms, chopped**
- ☐ **1 cup ricotta cheese**
- ☐ **15-ounce can tuna in mineral water, drained and reserving liquid**
- ☐ **2 tablespoons finely chopped fresh dill**
- ☐ **freshly ground black pepper**

SAUCE
- ☐ **1 tablespoon polyunsaturated margarine**
- ☐ **2 tablespoons all-purpose flour**
- ☐ **½ cup reserved tuna liquid**
- ☐ **1 teaspoon lemon juice**
- ☐ **1 cup low-fat plain yogurt**
- ☐ **freshly ground black pepper**

1   To make filling, cook onion and garlic in a non-stick skillet until onion softens. Add mushrooms and cook 3-4 minutes longer. Combine ricotta and tuna in a bowl. Mix in onion-mushroom mixture and dill. Season with pepper.
2   Cut lasagna sheets in half. Spoon filling down the center of each half sheet and roll up. Place in a lightly greased ovenproof dish.
3   To make sauce, melt margarine in a small saucepan. Stir in flour and cook for 1 minute. Stir in reserved tuna liquid and lemon juice and cook until sauce thickens. Remove from heat and set aside to cool.

Mix in yogurt and heat gently. Season with pepper.
4   Pour sauce over pasta and top with Parmesan cheese. Bake at 350° for 30 minutes, or until top is golden. Serve garnished with fresh dill if desired.

300 calories per serving

Fat	13.3 g	medium
Cholesterol	80 mg	low
Fiber	1.4 g	medium
Sodium	618 mg	high

COOK'S TIP
If you prefer, you can use tuna canned in brine, but avoid tuna canned in oil because of high calorie content. If using tuna in brine, you may wish to use 3 tablespoons stock and 3 tablespoons tuna liquid so that it is not too salty. This, however, will depend upon your own taste.

❖

SPINACH AND SALMON TIMBALES

Serves 4

- ☐ **1 bunch spinach (about 2 pounds), washed**

FILLING
- ☐ **7-ounce can salmon, drained**
- ☐ **⅓ cup ricotta cheese**
- ☐ **2 tablespoons finely chopped chives**
- ☐ **2 tablespoons finely chopped fresh parsley**
- ☐ **1 egg, lightly beaten**
- ☐ **freshly ground black pepper**

1   Boil, steam or microwave spinach until just wilted. Drain and allow to cool.
2   Select the largest spinach leaves and use to line four very lightly greased individual ramekins of about 1 cup capacity. Leave some of the leaves overhanging the top.
3   To make filling, squeeze as much liquid as possible from remaining spinach and chop finely. In a food processor or blender, combine salmon, ricotta, chives, parsley and egg. Process until smooth. Mix in chopped spinach and season with pepper.
4   Spoon mixture into prepared ramekins. Fold spinach leaves over the top. Bake at 350° for 30 minutes or until set.

156 calories per serving

Fat	9.1 g	low
Cholesterol	123 mg	medium
Fiber	2.9 g	high
Sodium	544 mg	medium

Spinach and Salmon Timbales

Best-Ever Hamburgers

- [ ] **2 teaspoons polyunsaturated oil**
- [ ] **1 onion, sliced**
- [ ] **1 teaspoon curry powder**
- [ ] **³/₄ cup low-fat plain yogurt**
- [ ] **1 tablespoon chopped mango chutney**

1   Poach chicken pieces in a saucepan with wine, water, onion and black pepper for 30-35 minutes, or until tender. Do not overcook the chicken or it will toughen. Remove chicken from poaching liquid and chill. Strain liquid and refrigerate to use for stock later .

2   To make dressing, heat oil in a skillet. Cook onion and curry powder until onion softens. Transfer to a small bowl and mix in yogurt and mango chutney.

3   Place cold chicken, peppers and celery in a bowl. Pour dressing over and gently mix to coat chicken pieces. Chill until ready to serve. Just before serving, peel and slice mango and use to garnish the salad.

649 calories per serving

Fat	17.3 g	medium
Cholesterol	195 mg	medium
Fiber	3.7 g	high
Sodium	354 mg	medium

❖

BEST-EVER HAMBURGERS

Just because you are watching what you eat, there is no need to give up all the best things in life. These delicious hamburgers will satisfy all the family - and you needn't tell them just how healthy they are!

Serves 6

- [ ] **1¹/₂ pounds lean ground beef**
- [ ] **1 onion, very finely chopped**
- [ ] **1 carrot, finely grated**
- [ ] **1 tablespoon Worcestershire sauce**
- [ ] **1 tablespoon tomato sauce**
- [ ] **dash chili sauce, according to taste**
- [ ] **¹/₂ teaspoon dried oregano**
- [ ] **¹/₂ teaspoon dried thyme**
- [ ] **freshly ground black pepper**
- [ ] **6 wholewheat rolls, split in half**
- [ ] **lettuce leaves**
- [ ] **6 slices beets**
- [ ] **6 slices peeled cucumber**
- [ ] **2 tomatoes, sliced**

1   Combine ground beef, onion, carrot, Worcestershire sauce, tomato sauce, chili sauce, oregano, thyme and pepper in a large bowl and mix well.

2   Wet hands and shape the mixture into six patties. Cook in a non-stick skillet for

❖

FRESH VEGETABLE SALAD WITH PEANUT SAUCE

Why not prepare our Indonesian-style salad well ahead of time and assemble it when you are ready to serve? It's great for casual summer entertaining and you can use your imagination in the combination of vegetables. Use fresh seasonal produce, if you can.

Serves 6

- [ ] **12 tiny new potatoes, scrubbed**
- [ ] **¹/₄ pound green beans, topped and tailed**
- [ ] **2 carrots, cut into thin strips**
- [ ] **¹/₂ Chinese cabbage, shredded**
- [ ] **cos lettuce leaves**
- [ ] **1 cucumber, cut into thin strips**
- [ ] **¹/₃ cup bean sprouts**

PEANUT SAUCE
- [ ] **1 clove garlic, crushed**
- [ ] **1 onion, chopped**
- [ ] **1 teaspoon chili sauce, or according to taste**
- [ ] **¹/₃ cup peanut butter**
- [ ] **¹/₂ cup water**
- [ ] **¹/₂ cup low-fat plain yogurt**
- [ ] **freshly ground black pepper**

1   Boil, steam or microwave potatoes until tender. Blanch beans, carrots and cabbage separately until barely tender. Drain and refresh under cold running water.

2   Line a large serving platter with cos lettuce leaves. Arrange all vegetables in mounds on top of lettuce.

3   To make sauce, cook garlic and onion in a non-stick skillet until onion softens. Add chili sauce, peanut butter and water. Mix well to combine and bring to a gentle boil. Stir in yogurt and season with pepper. Serve peanut sauce in a separate bowl on the vegetable platter.

232 calories per serving

Fat	9.5 g	low
Cholesterol	2 mg	low
Fiber	8.3 g	high
Sodium	123 mg	low

❖

CHILLED CURRIED CHICKEN SALAD

Serves 6

- [ ] **6 chicken pieces, skin removed**
- [ ] **1 cup dry white wine**
- [ ] **1 cup water**
- [ ] **1 small onion, chopped**
- [ ] **freshly ground black pepper**
- [ ] **¹/₂ green pepper, diced**
- [ ] **¹/₂ red pepper, diced**
- [ ] **2 stalks celery**
- [ ] **1 mango, for garnish**

5-6 minutes, pressing down with a spatula.

3   To assemble burgers, toast rolls. On bottom half of each roll, place lettuce, burger, beets, cucumber and tomato. Top with remaining half roll.

400 calories per serving

Fat	*15.3 g*	*medium*
Cholesterol	*79 mg*	*low*
Fiber	*7.6 g*	*high*
Sodium	*473 mg*	*medium*

❖

SALMON AND VEGETABLE LOAF

Serves 6

- ☐ **1 tablespoon polyunsaturated oil**
- ☐ **1 onion, chopped**
- ☐ **1 stalk celery, chopped**
- ☐ **¹/₂ red pepper, diced**
- ☐ **15-ounce can salmon, drained**
- ☐ **¹/₂ cup fresh wholewheat bread crumbs**
- ☐ **1 tablespoon snipped chives**
- ☐ **1 tablespoon chopped fresh parsley**
- ☐ **freshly ground black pepper**
- ☐ **2 egg whites, stiffly beaten**

1   Heat oil in a skillet and cook onion, celery and pepper for 2-3 minutes, or until onion softens.

2   Combine salmon, bread crumbs, chives, parsley and onion mixture in a bowl. Season with pepper. Fold egg whites lightly into salmon mixture.

3   Spoon into a lightly greased and lined loaf pan. Bake at 350° for 45 minutes, or until firm. Stand 10 minutes before turning out. Cut into slices to serve.

159 calories per serving

Fat	*9.0 g*	*low*
Cholesterol	*127 mg*	*medium*
Fiber	*0.8 g*	*low*
Sodium	*438 mg*	*medium*

❖

STIR-FRY NOODLES WITH PORK AND VEGETABLES

Serves 6

- ☐ **¹/₂ pound Oriental flat noodles**
- ☐ **1 tablespoon polyunsaturated oil or peanut oil**
- ☐ **1 clove garlic, finely chopped**
- ☐ **1 red chili, seeded and chopped**
- ☐ **1 onion, sliced**
- ☐ **1 teaspoon ground turmeric**
- ☐ **¹/₂ teaspoon ground cumin**
- ☐ **¹/₂ teaspoon ground coriander**
- ☐ **2 stalks celery, cut into thin strips**
- ☐ **1 bell pepper, cut into thin strips**
- ☐ **6 ounces pork fillet, cut into strips**
- ☐ **¹/₃ cup cubed tofu**
- ☐ **¹/₃ cup bean sprouts**

GARNISH

- ☐ **1 tablespoon chopped fresh coriander**
- ☐ **¹/₄ cup slivered almonds**

1   Cook noodles in boiling water according to package directions. Drain and set aside.

2   Heat oil in a wok or skillet. Add garlic, chili, onion, turmeric, cumin and coriander. Stir-fry for 3-4 minutes. Mix in celery and pepper, and cook 2-3 minutes longer. Remove vegetables with a slotted spoon and set aside. Stir-fry pork for 4-5 minutes, or until just tender. Return onion mixture to wok. Add tofu, bean sprouts and noodles, and cook for 2-3 minutes to heat through. Transfer to a warm serving plate, and sprinkle with coriander and almonds.

165 calories per serving

Fat	*7.4 g*	*low*
Cholesterol	*18 mg*	*low*
Fiber	*3.0 g*	*high*
Sodium	*45 mg*	*low*

Stir-fry Noodles with Pork and Vegetables, Fresh Vegetable Salad with Peanut Sauce, Chilled Curried Chicken Salad and Salmon and Vegetable Loaf

MIDDLE EASTERN POCKET SANDWICHES

Pita bread makes a wonderful container for holding all kinds of your favorite fillings. We have filled our pocket bread with refreshing cucumber salad, exotic lettuce leaves and succulent chunks of lean roast lamb. For a change, try serving this delicious combination as an open sandwich on fresh rye, wholewheat or grain bread.

Serves 4

- [ ] **4 wholewheat pita breads**
- [ ] **mignonette lettuce leaves**
- [ ] **1 pound lean roast lamb, cut into ¹/₂-inch chunks**
- [ ] **fresh mint sprigs for garnish**

CUCUMBER AND YOGURT SALAD
- [ ] **1 cucumber, peeled and chopped**
- [ ] **3 green onions, finely chopped**
- [ ] **¹/₂ cup finely chopped fresh mint leaves**
- [ ] **1 cup low-fat plain yogurt**
- [ ] **1 tablespoon lemon juice**
- [ ] **¹/₂ teaspoon chili sauce, or according to taste**
- [ ] **freshly ground black pepper**

Middle Eastern Pocket Sandwiches, Avocado and Chicken on Pumpernickel and Smoked Salmon on Rye

1 Cut pita breads in half and carefully open. Line each half with lettuce leaves.
2 To make salad, place cucumber, green onions and mint in a bowl. Mix together yogurt, lemon juice and chili sauce. Pour over cucumber salad and fold gently to combine. Season with pepper.
3 Spoon salad and lamb into pita pockets. Serve with fresh mint sprigs.

426 calories per serving

Fat	11.5 g	medium
Cholesterol	142 mg	medium
Fiber	5.4 g	high
Sodium	489 mg	medium

COOK'S TIP

Choose a selection of open sandwiches to make a wonderful informal lunch for a group of people or treat yourself with a favorite combination of fillings. If you use margarine, spread it very sparingly; if using a dressing or mayonnaise, there is no need to use margarine or a spread as well There are many combinations of fresh ingredients you might like to try. It may inspire you to experiment with some combinations of your own.

SMOKED SALMON ON RYE

Makes 4 sandwiches

- [ ] **¹/₄ pound thinly sliced smoked salmon**
- [ ] **4 slices rye bread**
- [ ] **juice of ¹/₂ lemon**
- [ ] **¹/₂ red onion, cut into thin slices**
- [ ] **8 thin slices cucumber**
- [ ] **4 teaspoons drained capers**
- [ ] **4 thin slices lemon**
- [ ] **freshly ground black pepper**
- [ ] **fresh dill sprigs for garnish**

1 Arrange salmon on bread slices and sprinkle with a little lemon juice.
2 Place onion on salmon. Arrange cucumber, capers and lemon slices attractively on top. Season with plenty of freshly ground black pepper and garnish with dill sprigs. Serve with a tossed green salad.

143 calories per serving

Fat	3.9 g	low
Cholesterol	26 mg	low
Fiber	3.8 g	high
Sodium	1132 mg	high

AVOCADO AND CHICKEN ON PUMPERNICKEL

Makes 4 sandwiches

- [ ] **1 large avocado, peeled and seeded**
- [ ] **juice of 1 lemon**
- [ ] **¹/₄ pound snow pea sprouts**
- [ ] **4 slices pumpernickel bread**
- [ ] **fresh mint sprigs for garnish**

CHICKEN SALAD
- [ ] **1 cup chopped cooked chicken**
- [ ] **2 shallots, finely chopped**
- [ ] **1 tablespoon pine nuts**
- [ ] **1 teaspoon finely chopped fresh mint**
- [ ] **2 tablespoons low-fat mayonnaise**

1 Cut avocado into 12 slices and sprinkle with lemon juice.
2 To make chicken salad, combine chicken, shallots, pine nuts, mint and mayonnaise in a bowl.
3 Divide snow pea sprouts between bread slices and top with chicken salad. Arrange three avocado slices on top of chicken salad and garnish with mint sprigs.

410 calories per serving

Fat	26.8 g	high
Cholesterol	100 mg	low
Fiber	5.9 g	high
Sodium	341 mg	medium

CLASSIC LIGHT

LASAGNA

Serves 4

- [ ] **2 teaspoons olive oil**
- [ ] **1 onion, chopped**
- [ ] **1 clove garlic, crushed**
- [ ] **$\frac{1}{4}$ pound lean ground beef**
- [ ] **10-ounce can soy beans, drained**
- [ ] **15-ounce can peeled tomatoes, undrained and mashed**
- [ ] **1 tablespoon tomato paste**
- [ ] **$1\frac{1}{2}$ tablespoons chopped fresh basil**
- [ ] **$\frac{1}{4}$ teaspoon dried oregano leaves**
- [ ] **$\frac{1}{4}$ teaspoon sugar**
- [ ] **6 sheets instant spinach lasagna noodles**
- [ ] **$\frac{1}{2}$ cup ricotta cheese**
- [ ] **$\frac{1}{2}$ cup cottage cheese**
- [ ] **1 egg white**
- [ ] **1 tablespoon grated Parmesan cheese**

1 Heat oil in a skillet. Cook onion and garlic for 2-3 minutes. Add beef and cook over medium heat until well browned. Combine soy beans, tomatoes, tomato paste, 2 teaspoons basil, oregano and sugar. Drain pan of any juices and stir in tomato mixture. Simmer, uncovered, for 15 minutes or until sauce thickens slightly.
2 Spread half the meat mixture over the bottom of a 10 x 7-inch ovenproof dish. Top with three lasagna sheets, placed side by side. Repeat with remaining meat mixture and lasagna sheets.
3 Place ricotta cheese, cottage cheese and egg white in a food processor or blender and process until smooth. Spread cheese mixture over lasagna in dish. Top with Parmesan cheese and remaining basil. Bake at 375° for 35-40 minutes or until tender.

262 calories per serving

Fat	*10.0 g*	*low*
Cholesterol	*44 mg*	*low*
Fiber	*4.9 g*	*high*
Sodium	*456 mg*	*medium*

HOW WE'VE CUT FAT AND CALORIES

✧ We have used lean ground beef for the filling.

✧ We alternated a layer of vegetable with the meat to keep the fiber high and the calories low.

✧ Instead of the usual rich Bechamel cheese sauce on top, we made a lighter version based on skim milk and cornstarch.

PRINCIPLES OF WEIGHT
CONTROL

Plan to lose weight slowly - 1 to 2 pounds per week is ideal.
Weigh yourself once a week in the same clothes, on the same
scales, at about the same time.

FACTS FOR SLIMMERS

Follow a sensible diet, including breakfast, lunch and dinner. If you like to snack, include them but as part of your daily allowance. Don't skip meals – you will just get hungry and eat more (or too much) at the next meal.

Base your diet on breads and grain-based foods, fruit and vegetables, lean meats, low-fat dairy foods, lean poultry, eggs, cheese, fish and legumes. Avoid too much fat (butter, margarine, oil, cream, salad dressing), sugar, salt and alcohol. Take advantage of low-calorie products available – sugar-free soft drinks, cordials, low - calorie jellies, oil-free salad dressings.

Drink plenty of water.

Be aware that you may break your diet from time to time. If you do, don't use it as an excuse to binge. Just get straight back to it. Bingeing will only make you depressed and angry with yourself for failing. A binge-and-diet pattern is not healthy for your body.

Accept that you will crave some ice cream, chocolate, cake or sweets. Satisfy the craving by having one serving and make sure you enjoy it. One serving will not make you put on weight, but half an ice cream container or a box of chocolates may well do!

Be realistic about your body shape. Not everyone can be a Jane Fonda or Princess Di! We all have a different body shape and no amount of dieting will change that.

To lose 1 pound of body fat, you must burn off some 3500 calories. This is equivalent to cutting back on 500 calories each day by eating less food or doing more exercise. Over a week, just this small deficit will produce a loss of 1 pound of fat, as well as associated water loss.

SUCCESSFUL WEIGHT LOSS

Losing weight involves more than just getting rid of fat! Certainly this is important, but successful dieting also means keeping healthy and happy, having enough energy for work and home life, and, most importantly, changing your eating habits so that the weight you lose will stay off forever. You therefore need to follow a plan that fits in with your food preferences and your lifestyle and one that does not need special dietary foods. You may need to adjust your eating behavior (the way you eat) as well as increasing your exercise level. Exercise helps burn fat faster by raising metabolic rate and by increasing lean muscle.

Weight does not come off in a straight, steady drop. It tends to hover on a "plateau", then fall dramatically in one step. If you weigh yourself regularly, it's often helpful to plot your weight on a graph and actually "see" how your weight loss is progressing.

Some dieters find a diet diary keeps them on track with their food plan. Simply write down everything you eat and drink over the day and review it at the end of the day. Just knowing that you have to write it down keeps you from snacking on the wrong food.

HOW TO START

First of all decide if you need to lose weight. The easiest way is to look at yourself in the mirror or to try on last year's clothes. If you look too fat or your clothes are tighter than they were last year, you need to diet. A more accurate way is to consult height and weight charts. If your weight falls outside the healthy weight range, it's time to diet. Remember that going on a diet unnecessarily and losing too much weight can be just as hazardous as putting on too much, and can disturb your metabolic rate.

Don't forget to check with your doctor before you embark on any diet.

HEIGHT AND WEIGHT CHARTS

These healthy weight ranges are based on data from a number of studies which show acceptable weights consistent with lowest mortality (from Garrow, 1981, Classification of Obesity, Churchill Livingstone).

FOR WOMEN AND MEN 18 YEARS AND OLDER

HEIGHT (without shoes)		BODY WEIGHT (in light clothing without shoes)
4 ft	7 ins	
4	8	86 - 88 lbs
4	9	86 - 110 lbs
4	9½	90 - 114 lbs
4	10	95 - 117 lbs
4	11	97 - 121 lbs
5	0	99 - 123 lbs
5	1	101 - 128 lbs
5	1½	103 - 130 lbs
5	2	108 - 134 lbs
5	3	110 - 136 lbs
5	4	112 - 141 lbs
5	4½	114 - 145 lbs
5	5	119 - 147 lbs
5	6	121 - 152 lbs
5	7	123 - 156 lbs
5	8	128 - 158 lbs
5	8½	130 - 163 lbs
5	9	134 - 167 lbs
5	10	136 - 169 lbs
5	11	139 - 174 lbs
6	0	143 - 178 lbs
6	½	145 - 183 lbs
6	1	150 - 187 lbs
6	2	152 - 189 lbs
6	3	156 - 194 lbs
6	4	158 - 198 lbs
6	4½	164 - 202 lbs
6	5	165 - 207 lbs
6	6	169 - 211 lbs
6	7	172 - 216 lbs

METRIC WEIGHT CONVERTER

176 - 220 lbs	127
kg	**st lbs**
1.0	2 lbs
6.4	1 st
10	1 st 8 lbs
20	3 st 2 lbs
40	6 st 4 lbs
44	6 st 13 lbs
46	7 st 4 lbs
48	7 st 8 lbs
50	7 st 13 lbs
52	8 st 3 lbs
54	8 st 7 lbs
56	8 st 12 lbs
58	9 st 2 lbs
60	9 st 6 lbs
62	9 st 11 lbs
64	10 st 2 lbs
66	10 st 6 lbs
68	10 st 10 lbs
70	11 st 1 lb
72	11 st 5 lbs
74	11 st 10 lbs
76	12 st
78	12 st 4 lbs
80	12 st 9 lbs
82	12 st 13 lbs
84	13 st 4 lbs
86	13 st 8 lbs
88	13 st 13 lbs
90	14 st
92	14 st 4 lbs
95	14 st 11 lbs
100	

DIETER'S
FRIENDS

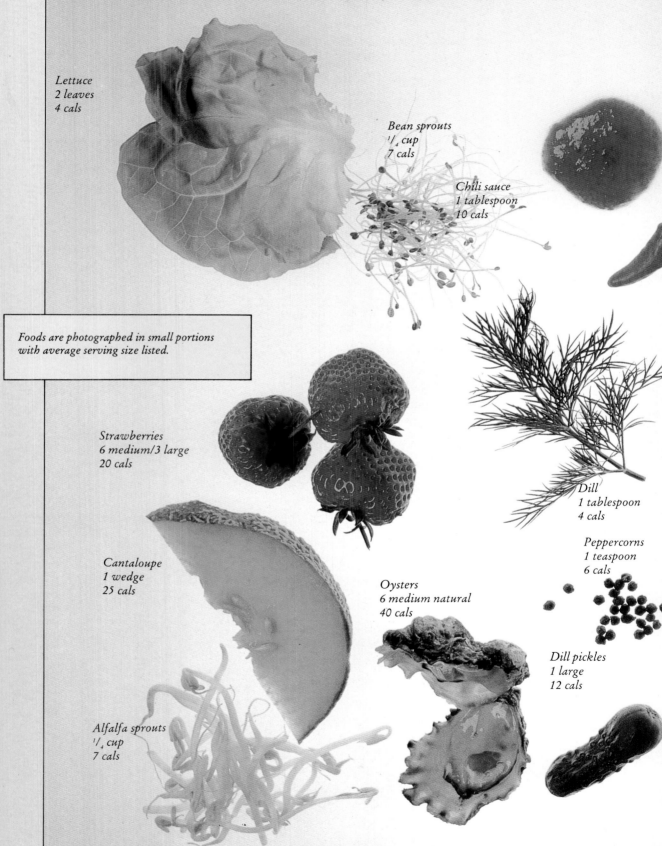

Lettuce
2 leaves
4 cals

Bean sprouts
¹/₄ cup
7 cals

Chili sauce
1 tablespoon
10 cals

Foods are photographed in small portions
with average serving size listed.

Strawberries
6 medium/3 large
20 cals

Dill
1 tablespoon
4 cals

Peppercorns
1 teaspoon
6 cals

Cantaloupe
1 wedge
25 cals

Oysters
6 medium natural
40 cals

Dill pickles
1 large
12 cals

Alfalfa sprouts
¹/₄ cup
7 cals

Calorie counters are fine, but when you can actually see foods and their calorie count, it makes more sense more quickly. Here are the lightest, lowest-calorie foods that you should try to include as often as possible with your meals. You can eat as much as you want of them and never put on weight!

Parsley (and other fresh herbs)
1 tablespoon
4 cals

Pepper
¹/₂ large
11 cals

Buttermilk
¹/₂ glass
45 cals

Cucumber
3 slices
5 cals

Shrimp
1 large
15 cals

Curry powder
1 teaspoon
7 cals

Celery
1 piece
5 cals

Tomato
1 small
22 cals

Mushrooms
1 medium
2 cals

Lime
1 small
17 cals

Artificial sweeteners
1 sweetener
negligible

HOW TO COUNT FAT

Counting calories is out but counting fat is in! Why? Because counting the fat content of foods makes dieting simpler and easier.

DIETING MADE EASY
At 9 calories per gram, fat has double the calories of protein and carbohydrate and is therefore our most concentrated energy source. So any food high in fat is literally "fattening" and must be avoided or restricted while losing weight. Reducing dietary fat is also in line with international nutrition guidelines for maintaining a healthy body.

Our fat counter tells you the fat content of a wide variety of foods and will assist you in avoiding foods with high levels of fat.

To maintain a nutritious diet while restricting fat, remember to follow these simple guidelines.

EAT MOST
Breads, cereals, fruit, vegetables (except avocados), pasta (avoid fatty sauces), rice (not fried), flour, legumes.

EAT MODERATELY
Lean meats, poultry (no skin), fish, eggs, dairy foods (preferably low-fat varieties of milk, cheese, yogurt).

EAT LEAST
Butter, margarine, oil, salad dressings, cream, sour cream, mayonnaise, nuts, bacon, pâté, salami, fried food, meat fat, fatty sauces.

WHAT ABOUT ALCOHOL?
Alcohol itself contains no fat but is still a high source of calories, following closely behind fat at 7 calories per gram. It is therefore best restricted or avoided entirely for successful weight loss.

Potato, boiled or baked in jacket 0 fat 76 calories

Potato, roasted in oil 10 g fat 164 calories

Potato chips 14 g fat 238 calories

Potato chips 36 g fat 543 calories

HANDY
FAT COUNTER

This chart lists average values for food eaten
without adding fat. Derived from Food Composition Tables
and analyses supplied by manufacturers and fast food chains.
Negligible = less than 0.5 grams fat
Trace = less than 0.1 grams fat

BEVERAGES

Alcohol – Beer, wine, sherry, gin, rum, whisky, vodka	0
Cappuccino	2.4
Cocoa – hot, made with milk, 1 cup	9.1
Coffee – no milk	0
with milk	1.2
Cordial	0
Fruit Juice	0
Milkshake – chocolate, 1 cup	17.0
Tea – no milk	0
with milk	1.2

BREADS

Bread white, 1 slice	0.7
mixed grain, 1 slice	0.8
wholewheat, 1 slice	0.8
rye, 1 slice	0.7
raisin or fruit, 1 slice	1.2
Bagel, 1 whole	2.0
Croissant, 1 whole	14.0
Crumpet, 1	0.6
Frankfurter roll	3.0
Flat bread	2.0
Hamburger bun	3.0
Matzo, 1 slice	0.6
Muffin, English	1.1
Muffin, American, blueberry	10.3
Rolls, all varieties	1.6
Taco shells/tostado	2.2

BISCUITS/COOKIES/CRACKERS

SAVORY

Plain, 1	1.0
Plain salted, 1	0.7
Rye cracker, 1	negligible
Whole wheat, 1	0.7
Water Biscuits, 1	negligible

SWEET

Anzac, 1	4.8
Carob, 1	5.3
Chocolate chip, 1	3.0
Chocolate coated,	2.8
Chocolate flavored, 1 and cream filled, 1	3.3
Fruit and nuts, 1	2.9
Ginger, 1	1.7
Iced, 1	1.5
Marshmallow, 1	2.7
Nuts, 1	2.8
Plain, 1	1.6
Oatmeal, 1	2.3
Shortbread, 1	3.0
Filled wafers, 1	2.2

CEREALS – BREAKFAST

All Bran, 1/2 cup	1.5
Corn flakes, 1 cup	0.5
Muesli, toasted, 2 tablespoons	5.0
Oatmeal, 1 cup cooked	2.6
Oats, instant, 1 package	1.7
Rice bubbles, 1 cup	0.4
Unprocessed bran, 1 heaped tablespoon	0.3
Wheatflake biscuits, 2	0.8
Wheat germ, 1 tablespoon	0.9

CAKES AND PASTRIES

Carrot cake, 1 slice	18.0
Chocolate eclair, 1	17.6
Cupcake, 1	6.0
Danish pastry, 1	15.2
Donut, 1	7.0
Fruitcake, 1 slice	7.9
Jam tart, 1	6.7
Lamington, 1	8.7
Scone, 1	3.0
Sponge cake, 1 slice	4.3
Vanilla slice, 1	12.0
Muesli slice, 1	17.9

CHEESES

Per 1 ounce serving	
Brie	8.7
Camembert	8.0
Cheddar, full fat	10.1
reduced fat	7.1
Cheshire	9.8
Cottage Cheese	2.8
Creamed Cottage Cheese	1.7
low-fat	0.7
Cream Cheese	10.2
Edam	8..4
Feta, full-fat	7.5
reduced-fat	4.4
Gloucester	10.3
Mozzarella	6.9
Parmesan	9.5
Ricotta	3.4
Swiss	9.0

CONFECTIONS/CANDY

Butterscotch, 1 average piece	0.5
Caramel, 1 cube	0.9
Chocolate, plain dark, 1 1/2 ounces	15.3
milk, 1 1/2 ounces	15.0
Jelly beans, 4-5	negligible
Gumdrops, 4-5	negligible
Marshmallow, plain	trace
Popcorn, plain 3 ounces	3.5
Toffee, mixed	18.4

DESSERTS

Apple pie, 1/6 of 8" pie	16.2
Apple strudel, 1 slice	12.4
Cheesecake, 1 slice	36.6
Custard tart, 1	17.6
Ice cream, gourmet, rich, 1 serving	15.5
Ice cream, 1 serving	6.0
Ice confection, 1 serving	5.0
Ice confection, low-fat, 1 serving	1.0

Lemon meringue pie, 1 serving,
$\frac{1}{8}$ of pie | 13.1
Pecan pie, 1 serving, $\frac{1}{8}$ of pie | 16.8

EGGS
1 medium boiled/poached | 5.6
1 omelet, 2 eggs, plain | 22.6
Scrambled egg,
1 egg + milk + butter | 12.4
1 egg white | trace
1 egg yolk | 5.2

FAT
Butter, 1 teaspoon | 4.0
Cream, 1 tablespoon | 7.6
Margarine, 1 tablespoon | 4.0
Mayonnaise, 1 tablespoon | 15.0
Low-fat Mayonnaise,
1 tablespoon | 8.8
Oil, polyunsaturated/olive,
1 tablespoon | 18.9
Reduced-fat spread,
1 teaspoon | 2.0
Sour cream (35% fat),
1 tablespoon | 7.0
Light sour cream (18% fat),
1 tablespoon | 3.6

FISH
Crab, canned, $\frac{1}{2}$ cup | 2.2
Fish, 1 fillet steamed/baked | 2.3
Fish, 1 portion,
battered/deep-fried | 22.8
Fish cake, 1 | 11.7
Herring, canned, 2 small | 13.1
Oysters, 12 | 1.8
Salmon, smoked,
3 small pieces | 4.7
canned, $\frac{1}{2}$ cup | 9.3
Sardines, 4-5 small | 13.4
Tuna, 3 ounces in oil | 19.5
3 ounces in water | 5.8

FRUITS
Fresh, canned, frozen,
dried, per serving | negligible
Avocado, 1 medium | 30.0

MEATS

BEEF
Boneless, average all cuts,
cooked, 75% trim, 1 cup | 13.8
Filet steak, grilled | 6.8
Ground, cooked | 20.6
Rump, grilled | 17.0
Topside lean roast | 2.6

CHICKEN
Boneless, baked, lean and
skin, $\frac{1}{2}$ chicken | 43.6
Breast quarter, rotisseried,
lean and skin | 12.3
Chicken breast, baked,
no skin, $\frac{1}{2}$ breast | 3.8
Chicken drumstick, baked
lean with skin, 2 small | 15.0

PORK
Boneless, average all cuts,
cooked 75% trim, 1 cup | 10.7
Forequarter chop, grilled,
75% trim, 1 chop | 16.4
Baked leg roast, 75% trim ,
1 slice | 4.0

LAMB
Boneless, average all cuts,
75% trimmed,
cooked 5 ounces | 16.2
Lamb leg roast, 75% trim,
$1\frac{1}{2}$-ounce slice | 3.1
Lamb chump chop, grilled,
75% trim, 1 chop | 6.4
Lamb cutlet, grilled,
75% trim, 1 ounce | 4.5
Lamb shoulder, baked,
75% trim, 1 slice | 2.8

VEAL
Leg steak, fried, lean and fat,
1 steak | 2.6
Veal leg, baked, lean and fat,
1 slice | 0.7
Veal loin chop, grilled, lean,
1 chop | 1.4

PROCESSED MEATS
Sausages, beef, 2 thick | 24.3
2 thin | 16.6
Sausages, pork, 2 thick | 25.4
2 thin | 17.3
Chicken Roll, 1 slice | 2.3
Cabanossi, 1 slice | 9.5
Devon, 1 slice | 5.3
Frankfurters, boiled, 2 | 23.8
Ham, lean, 1 slice | 0.8
Liverwurst, 1 ounce | 7.4
Polish salami, 1-ounce slice | 5.3
Strasbourg, 1-ounce slice | 5.8
Salami, 1-ounce slice | 11.3

MILK/YOGURT
Whole milk, 3 ounces | 3.9
Skim milk, 3 ounces | negligible
Flavored milk, 3 ounces | 3.7
Butter milk, 3 ounces | 0.8
Yogurt, 6-ounce carton,
fruit and full-fat | 7.0

6-ounce tub, fruit
and low-fat | negligible
6-ounce tub, plain and full-fat | 7.0
6-ounce tub, plain
and low-fat | negligible

PASTA/RICE
Egg noodles, 1 cup, boiled | 2.0
Fried rice, $\frac{1}{2}$ cup | 7.2
Macaroni, boiled, 1 cup | 0.8
Rice, boiled, 1 cup | 0.3
Spaghetti, boiled, 1 cup | 0.8

SALAD DRESSINGS
Coleslaw, 1 tablespoon | 7.1
French, 1 tablespoon | 4.6
Thousand Island,
1 tablespoon | 7.1
Low calorie, 1 tablespoon | 0
Italian, 1 tablespoon | 1.0

SAUCES/GRAVIES/CHUTNEYS
BBQ sauce, 1 tablespoon | negligible
Cheese sauce, 2 tablespoons | 6.1
Chutney, 1 tablespoon | trace
Chili sauce, 1 tablespoon | negligible
Gravy, with fat, $\frac{1}{4}$ cup | 5.5
Hollandaise, $\frac{1}{4}$ cup | 18.5
Soy sauce | negligible
Tomato sauce, 1 tablespoon | negligible
Tartare sauce, 1 tablespoon | 6.1
White sauce, 2 tablespoons | 4.0

SNACK FOODS
Almonds, roasted/salted, 26 | 17.0
Cashews, roasted, 15 | 14.2
Cheese flavored
snack, 1 small packet | 9.8
Corn chips, 1 small packet | 11.6
Olives, green, 2 medium | 1.6
black, 2 large | 4.0
Pork rind snack,
1 small packet | 7.1
Potato crisps, 1 small packet | 11.7
Potato straws, 1 small packet | 11.0
Pretzels, 20 sticks | 0.9
Pecans, 12 halves, | 9.1
Peanuts, 36-38 | 14.6

SPREADS
Cheese spread, 20 g | 0
Fish paste, 1 teaspoon | negligible
Honey | 0
Jam and other preserves | trace
Meat paste, 1 teaspoon | 0.7
Peanut butter, 1 tablespoon | 10.4

SOUPS

Cream of asparagus with milk, 1 cup	8.2
Beef broth, 1 cup	0.5
Chicken noodle with water, 1 cup	2.5
Minestrone, 1 cup	2.8
Cream of mushroom with milk, 1 cup	13.6
French onion	5.8
Cream of tomato with milk	6.0
Vegetable with beef broth	1.9

TAKEOUT FOODS/FAST FOODS

Big Mac	30.6
Cheese sandwich	5.3
Cheeseburger	16.0
Crumbed chicken	30.2
Dim Sim	6.0
Filet-O-Fish	21.5
French fries	20.2
Hamburger, plain	17.5
Meat pie, 1 individual	23.7
1 party	7.8
Pasty, 1	25.4
Potato chips, 6 ounces	32.6
Potato scallop, 1	21.3
Sausage roll, 1 large	22.7
1 party	8.4
Spring roll, 1	17.0
Thick shake, chocolate, vanilla, strawberry	8.9

VEGETABLES

Raw, steamed, baked with no fat	Negligible
Potato, baked, 1 medium	9.1
fried, 17-18 pieces	12.7
mashed, milk added, $\frac{1}{3}$ cup	0.5
hashed browns, $\frac{1}{2}$ cup	11.7
Creamed spinach, $\frac{1}{2}$ cup	3.0
Broccoli, frozen in butter sauce, $\frac{2}{3}$ cup	2.3

LEGUMES

Chick peas (garbanzo beans), $\frac{1}{2}$ cup	2.1
Kidney beans, red, $\frac{1}{2}$ cup	0.8
Lima beans, fresh, frozen or canned	negligible
Baked beans, $\frac{1}{4}$ cup	negligible
Peas, split and dried, boiled, 3 ounces	negligible

SALADS

Potato salad, 1 cup canned	12.4
Bean salad, 1 cup	10.1

COOK'S TIP

Make your own fast food. See our recipe for Best-Ever Hamburgers on page 34.

GREEN CUISINE

When you tempt your tastebuds with our light, refreshing and spicy selection of vegetable and salad recipes, you can safely come back for a second helping.

❖
CHINESE SESAME SLAW

Serves 6

- ☐ ¼ **pound snow peas, topped and tailed**
- ☐ ½ **Chinese cabbage, finely shredded**
- ☐ ⅔ **cup bean sprouts**
- ☐ **4 green onions, finely chopped**
- ☐ ½ **red pepper, cut into strips**
- ☐ ½ **cucumber, diced**
- ☐ **freshly ground black pepper**
- ☐ **2 tablespoons toasted sesame seeds**

DRESSING
- ☐ **2 teaspoons polyunsaturated oil**
- ☐ **1 teaspoon sesame oil**
- ☐ **2 tablespoons white wine vinegar**
- ☐ **1 tablespoon low-salt soy sauce**

1   Blanch snow peas and refresh under cold running water.
2   Combine cabbage, bean sprouts, green onions, pepper, cucumber and snow peas in a salad bowl.
3   To make dressing, place oils, vinegar and soy in a screwtop jar. Shake well to combine and pour over vegetables. Season with pepper and toss. Just before serving, sprinkle with pepper and sesame seeds.

99 calories per serving

Fat	6.1 g	low
Cholesterol	0 mg	low
Fiber	6.5 g	high
Sodium	144 mg	low

❖
CARROT AND GINGER SALAD

Serves 6

- ☐ **3 carrots, grated**
- ☐ ½ **cup sultanas**
- ☐ ¼ **cup alfalfa sprouts**
- ☐ **2 tablespoons finely chopped fresh chives**

DRESSING
- ☐ **1 tablespoon polyunsaturated oil**
- ☐ **2 tablespoons cider vinegar**
- ☐ **1 tablespoon green ginger wine**
- ☐ **1 teaspoon grated fresh ginger**

1   Combine carrots and sultanas in a bowl.
2   To make dressing, place oil, vinegar, wine and ginger in a screwtop jar. Shake well and pour over salad. Toss lightly to combine.
3   Place salad on a bed of alfalfa sprouts and serve garnished with chives.

63 calories per serving

Fat	1.6 g	low
Cholesterol	0 mg	low
Fiber	2.3 g	medium
Sodium	29 mg	low

❖
THAI-STYLE BEEF SALAD

Serves 6

- ☐ **1 pound piece fillet beef**
- ☐ **1 mignonette lettuce**
- ☐ ⅓ **to** ½ **cup bean sprouts**
- ☐ **1 red pepper, finely sliced**
- ☐ **1 cucumber, peeled, cut in half and sliced**
- ☐ **fresh sprigs coriander for garnish**

DRESSING
- ☐ **1 tablespoon polyunsaturated oil**
- ☐ **4 onions, chopped**
- ☐ **2 tablespoons lime juice**
- ☐ **1 clove garlic, crushed**
- ☐ **2 teaspoons Thai fish sauce**
- ☐ **1 red chili, seeded and finely chopped**

1   Remove all visible fat from meat. Brown on all sides in a non-stick skillet, by which time the meat should be cooked rare. Remove from pan and cool for about 30 minutes.
2   With a very sharp knife, slice meat thinly and place in a bowl.
3   To make dressing, place oil, onions, lime juice, garlic, fish sauce and chili in a screwtop jar. Shake well to combine and pour over meat. Cover and marinate for 1 hour.
4   Arrange lettuce, bean sprouts, pepper and cucumber attractively on a large serving platter. Top with beef and garnish with coriander.
NOTE: Thai fish sauce is available at most Oriental specialty food stores.

129 calories per serving

Fat	3.7 g	low
Cholesterol	56 mg	low
Fiber	3.0 g	high
Sodium	172 mg	low

❖
GARLIC, BEAN AND TOMATO CASSEROLE

Make an ideal main course of our simple and delicious casserole of beans and tomatoes by serving with bowls of plain yogurt and a little grated cheese.

Serves 4

- ☐ **1 tablespoon olive oil**
- ☐ **1 large onion, sliced**
- ☐ **2 cloves garlic, crushed**
- ☐ **15-ounce can peeled tomatoes, undrained and mashed**
- ☐ ½ **cup dry white wine**
- ☐ **2 tablespoons tomato paste**
- ☐ **1 tablespoon red wine vinegar**
- ☐ **2 teaspoons honey**
- ☐ **24-ounce can three-bean mix**
- ☐ **freshly ground black pepper**

1   Heat oil in a skillet. Cook onion and garlic for 2-3 minutes, or until onion softens. Add tomatoes, wine and tomato paste, and boil rapidly for 4-5 minutes until mixture reduces slightly. Stir in vinegar and honey.
2   Transfer tomato mixture to an ovenproof dish. Mix in beans and season with pepper. Bake at 350° for 30 minutes.

239 calories per serving

Fat	8.4 g	low
Cholesterol	0 mg	low
Fiber	9.2 g	high
Sodium	641 mg	high

Garlic, Bean and Tomato Casserole, Chinese Sesame Slaw, Thai-style Beef Salad and Carrot and Ginger Salad

NUTRITION TIP

Salads made from crispy, garden-fresh raw vegetables are an ideal way to keep the calories down and the fiber up. Try our tangy dressings with your favorite salad vegetables.

❖
MARINATED MUSHROOMS

These mushrooms make an excellent accompaniment to a meal or a low-calorie snack.

Serves 4

- ☐ **1 pound button mushrooms, stems removed**
- ☐ **¹/₂ red pepper, diced**
- ☐ **¹/₂ green pepper, diced**

DRESSING
- ☐ **1 clove garlic, crushed**
- ☐ **1 tablespoon polyunsaturated oil**
- ☐ **3 tablespoons red wine vinegar**
- ☐ **1 tablespoon finely chopped fresh parsley**
- ☐ **1 tablespoon finely chopped fresh chives**
- ☐ **freshly ground black pepper**

1   Place mushrooms and peppers in a bowl.
2   To make dressing, place garlic, oil, vinegar, parsley, chives and pepper in a screwtop jar. Shake well to combine and pour over mushrooms and peppers. Cover, refrigerate and marinate for about 2 hours before serving.

53 calories per serving

Fat	2.7 g	low
Cholesterol	0 mg	low
Fiber	3.7 g	high
Sodium	10 mg	low

❖
TOMATO AND BASIL SALAD

You might like to try a combination of cherry tomatoes and little yellow teardrop tomatoes to make this aromatic tomato salad look even more attractive.

Serves 6

- ☐ **1¹/₂ pounds ripe tomatoes, peeled and sliced**
- ☐ **4 tablespoons finely chopped fresh basil**
- ☐ **2 tablespoons grated Parmesan cheese**
- ☐ **freshly ground black pepper**

DRESSING
- ☐ **1 clove garlic, crushed**
- ☐ **1 tablespoon olive oil**
- ☐ **3 tablespoons white wine vinegar**

1   Arrange tomato slices overlapping on a serving platter and sprinkle with basil leaves.
2   To make dressing, place garlic, oil and vinegar in a screwtop jar. Shake well to

combine and sprinkle over tomatoes. Just before serving, sprinkle tomato salad with Parmesan cheese. Season with pepper.

55 calories per serving

Fat	3.6 g	low
Cholesterol	3 mg	low
Fiber	2.1 g	medium
Sodium	46 mg	low

❖
ITALIAN GREEN BEAN SALAD

Serves 4

- ☐ 1 pound green beans, topped and tailed
- ☐ 6 green onions, finely chopped
- ☐ 3 tomatoes, peeled and chopped
- ☐ 8 pitted ripe olives
- ☐ freshly ground black pepper

DRESSING
- ☐ 1 tablespoon olive oil
- ☐ 3 tablespoons lemon juice
- ☐ 1 clove garlic, crushed
- ☐ 1 tablespoon chopped fresh parsley
- ☐ 1 tablespoon finely chopped fresh chives
- ☐ 1 teaspoon finely chopped fresh rosemary
- ☐ 1 teaspoon finely chopped fresh thyme

1   Boil, steam or microwave beans until just tender. Refresh under cold running water.
2   Place beans, green onions, tomatoes and olives in a salad bowl.
3   To make dressing, place oil, lemon juice, garlic, parsley, chives, rosemary and thyme in a screwtop jar. Shake well to combine and pour over salad. Season with pepper and toss.

95 calories per serving

Fat	5.6 g	low
Cholesterol	0 mg	low
Fiber	6.7 g	high
Sodium	295 mg	low

❖
STIR-FRY VEGETABLES

Serves 6

- ☐ 1 tablespoon polyunsaturated oil
- ☐ 1 onion, sliced
- ☐ 1 clove garlic, crushed
- ☐ 1 teaspoon finely grated fresh ginger
- ☐ 1 carrot, thinly sliced
- ☐ 1 green pepper, diced
- ☐ 2 stalks celery, sliced
- ☐ 1/2 pound mushrooms, sliced
- ☐ 1/4 pound snow peas, topped and tailed
- ☐ 1/2 cabbage, shredded
- ☐ 8-ounce jar baby corn
- ☐ 1 tablespoon low-salt soy sauce

1   Heat oil until hot in a wok or skillet. Add onion, garlic and ginger and stir-fry for 2-3 minutes. Toss in carrot, pepper and celery, and cook for 4-5 minutes.
2   To vegetable mixture, add mushrooms and snow peas. Stir-fry for 1-2 minutes, or until snow peas are just tender. Stir in cabbage, corn and soy, and cook for 3-4 minutes. Serve immediately.

146 calories per serving

Fat	3.0 g	low
Cholesterol	0 mg	low
Fiber	10.5 g	high
Sodium	165 mg	low

❖
TOMATO, ZUCCHINI AND ONION BAKE

Serves 4

- ☐ 1 tablespoon olive oil
- ☐ 2 large onions, sliced into rings
- ☐ 1 clove garlic, crushed
- ☐ 1 green pepper, diced
- ☐ 1 teaspoon mixed Italian herbs
- ☐ 1/4 pound mushrooms, sliced
- ☐ 15-ounce can whole peeled tomatoes, undrained and mashed
- ☐ 1 tablespoon tomato paste
- ☐ 1 tablespoon cornstarch blended with 1/2 cup water
- ☐ 3 medium zucchini, thickly sliced

TOPPING
- ☐ 1/2 cup fresh bread crumbs
- ☐ 2 tablespoons grated cheddar cheese

1   Heat oil in a saucepan and cook onion, garlic, pepper and herbs for 2-3 minutes or until onion is soft. Add mushrooms and cook for 5 minutes.
2   Stir in tomatoes and tomato paste, and cook until mixture boils. Stir in cornstarch mixture and cook till sauce thickens.
3   Boil, steam or microwave zucchini until just tender. Place zucchini in a shallow ovenproof dish and pour tomato sauce over. Top with bread crumbs and cheese.
4   Place under a preheated grill and broil for 5 minutes or until top is golden.

173 calories per serving

Fat	6.2 g	low
Cholesterol	4 mg	low
Fiber	6.6 g	high
Sodium	133 mg	low

Far left: Italian Green Bean Salad, Tomato and Basil Salad and Marinated Mushrooms
Left: Tomato, Zucchini and Onion Bake, and Stir-fry Vegetables

VEGETABLE TIPS

✧ Cook vegetables in the shortest possible time (the microwave oven is ideal). This retains their valuable nutrients and keeps the color bright and texture crunchy.

✧ Do not thaw frozen vegetables; add directly to boiling water. Save vegetable water to use as a base for soups and gravies. This saves those vitamins and minerals being tossed down the sink!

✧ A platter of crisp raw vegetables is a good way to start off a dinner party. Guests can nibble on them or dunk into a dip in place of crackers. They are light and refreshing and won't spoil your appetite for the main course.

✧ Vegetables like mushrooms and eggplant can soak up large quantities of oil or butter during cooking. Rather than fry eggplant slices (say, for moussaka), brush with oil and place under the grill instead. Mushrooms can be sautéed in a little oil, covered and allowed to "steam" in their own natural water content.

✧ Taste your food before adding salt. Too many people automatically reach for the salt shaker without even tasting if the food is seasoned. Potatoes, tomatoes, eggs and fish may taste insipid for the first time without salt. Try adding chopped fresh parsley, dill or chives, or some freshly ground pepper.

✧ When eating out, ask for extra vegetables or choose vegetables plus salad.

✧ Try and buy fresh produce at a quality fruit and vegetable market. Seeing lots of vegetables at the peak of their ripeness is the best way to tempt yourself (and the family) into enjoying more of them.

✧ Remember, fruit and vegetables come into the "eat most" category when you are trying to maintain a nutritious diet while restricting fat.

❖
PUMPKIN SOUFFLE

Serves 4

- ☐ **1 tablespoon butter**
- ☐ **2 tablespoons all-purpose flour**
- ☐ **1¹/₂ cups skim milk**
- ☐ **4 eggs, separated**
- ☐ **1³/₄ cups canned pumpkin**
- ☐ **freshly ground black pepper**

1   Melt butter in a saucepan. Stir in flour and cook 1 minute. Gradually mix in milk. Cook until sauce boils and thickens. Remove pan from heat.

2   Beat egg yolks into white sauce and mix in canned pumpkin. Season with pepper.

3   Beat egg whites until stiff and fold into pumpkin mixture. Divide mixture between four individual soufflé dishes, with a capacity of about 1¹/₂ cups. Bake in a preheated oven at 400° for 20-25 minutes, or until soufflés are risen and golden. Serve immediately.

210 calories per serving

Fat	*10.7 g*	*medium*
Cholesterol	*261 mg*	*high*
Fiber	*0.7 g*	*low*
Sodium	*170 mg*	*low*

NUTRITION TIP

When trying recipes like these, which are higher in fat and sodium, balance out the rest of your meals for the day with less fat and salt. What you need is an overall, balanced nutritious food plan.

Above: Cheesy Vegetable Strudel and a Salad
Left: Pumpkin Soufflé

❖
CHEESY VEGETABLE STRUDEL

Serves 6

- ☐ **4 sheets filo pastry**
- ☐ **2 tablespoons olive oil**
- ☐ **2 tablespoons sesame seeds**

FILLING
- ☐ **2 teaspoons olive oil**
- ☐ **1 onion, chopped**
- ☐ **1 clove garlic, crushed**
- ☐ **$1/_3$ pound mushrooms, sliced**
- ☐ **1 bunch spinach (about 2 pounds), washed**
- ☐ **1 cup cottage cheese**
- ☐ **$3/_4$ cup crumbled feta cheese**
- ☐ **1 egg**
- ☐ **freshly ground black pepper**

1   To make filling, heat oil in a skillet. Cook onion and garlic 2-3 minutes. Add mushrooms and cook 3-4 minutes. Shake as much water as possible from spinach and add to pan. Cook until spinach starts to wilt. Squeeze to remove excess liquid. Combine with cheeses, egg and season with pepper.

2   Layer two sheets of filo pastry. Brush top sheet very lightly with oil, top with remaining two sheets and brush with oil.

3   Spread filling over pastry leaving about 1 inch around all edges. With the longest side towards you, fold in sides of pastry and roll up like a Swiss roll. Place on a cookie sheet and brush lightly with oil. Sprinkle with sesame seeds. Bake at 400° for 20-25 minutes, or until golden.

203 calories per serving

Fat	15.2 g	medium
Cholesterol	56 mg	low
Fiber	2.7 g	medium
Sodium	329 mg	medium

CLASSIC LIGHT

CAULIFLOWER AU GRATIN

Serves 4

- [ ] **1 small cauliflower, broken into flowerets**
- [ ] **1¹⁄₂ cups skim milk**
- [ ] **1¹⁄₂ tablespoons cornstarch blended with 3 tablespoons water**
- [ ] **1 teaspoon wholegrain mustard**
- [ ] **3 tablespoons low-fat plain yogurt**
- [ ] **freshly ground black pepper**
- [ ] **¹⁄₂ cup crushed cornflakes**
- [ ] **3 tablespoons grated low-fat cheese**
- [ ] **1 tablespoon butter, melted**
- [ ] **paprika**

1   Steam, boil or microwave cauliflower until just tender. Drain and set aside.
2   Place milk in a saucepan and cook over medium heat until almost at boiling point. Remove pan from heat and stir in cornstarch mixture. Return pan to heat and cook over medium heat until sauce boils and thickens, stirring constantly.
3   Combine mustard and yogurt. Remove sauce from heat and blend in yogurt mixture. Season with pepper. Spread half the sauce over the bottom of an ovenproof dish. Top with cauliflower and remaining sauce.
4   Combine cornflakes, cheese and butter. Sprinkle on top of cauliflower. Sprinkle with paprika and bake at 350° for 15-20 minutes or until golden brown.

198 calories per serving

Fat	6.4 g	low
Cholesterol	18 mg	low
Fiber	4.8 g	high
Sodium	307 mg	medium

HOW WE'VE CUT FAT AND CALORIES

✧ Avoid the butter-and-flour roux and make a light sauce based on skim milk and cornstarch.

✧ Add only a small quantity of cheese and mix it with wholewheat bread crumbs (or wheat germ or cornflake crumbs) to add crunch and color.

TOP
DRESSINGS

Our light and luscious dressings add a special touch. Use fresh herbs and spices and remember that safflower and sunflower oils are healthier than the usual salad oils.

CHILI DRESSING

Makes about 1 cup

1 red chili, seeded and finely chopped
1 clove garlic, crushed
2-3 tablespoons vinegar
2 tablespoons low-salt soy sauce
$1/_2$ cup sunflower or safflower oil
freshly ground black pepper

Place all ingredients in a screwtop jar. Season with pepper to taste. Shake well to combine before serving.

COOK'S TIP

If chili is unavailable, substitute 1 teaspoon chili sauce or $1/_4$ teaspoon ground chili.

SESAME DRESSING

Makes about 1 cup

1 tablespoon white wine vinegar
2 tablespoons sesame oil
$1/_2$ cup safflower or maize oil
freshly ground black pepper
1 tablespoon chopped fresh parsley
4 tablespoons toasted sesame seeds

Combine vinegar, oils and pepper in a screwtop jar. Shake well to combine. Just before serving, add parsley and sesame seeds. Shake again and pour over salad.

COOK'S TIP

To toast sesame seeds, place in a non-stick skillet and cook over moderate heat for 2-3 minutes or until just golden, stirring constantly. Take care not to burn. Allow to cool before adding to salad.

LIGHT VINAIGRETTE

Makes about 1 cup

$1/_2$ cup olive oil
2-3 tablespoons white wine vinegar
1 clove garlic, crushed
1 tablespoon Dijon-style mustard
4 tablespoons cold water
freshly ground black pepper

Place all ingredients in a screwtop jar. Season with pepper to taste. Shake well to combine before serving.

HERBED TOMATO DRESSING

Makes about $3/_4$ cup

$1/_2$ cup tomato juice
2 tablespoons lemon juice
1-2 tablespoons chopped fresh herbs (basil, parsley, chives or mint)
1 teaspoon Worcestershire sauce
freshly ground black pepper

Place all ingredients in a screwtop jar. Season with pepper to taste. Shake well to combine, then pour over salad just before serving.

FORGET
CRASH DIETS

Unfortunately there are no magic ways to shed weight. So don't be fooled by all those wonder diets, pills, formulas, herbal extracts, creams, exercise machines and garments promising quick weight loss.

WHY CRASH DIETS DON'T WORK

It took you more than a week to put on those extra pounds, so expect it to take at least that time and maybe more (depending on how much you've got to lose) to get it off.

You will lose weight on a crash diet in the short term but what you'll lose is water and lean muscle, not fat. "Crash" diets, high in protein and fat, lack carbohydrates, so that the muscle quickly uses up its glycogen stores first for energy. Every gram of glycogen contains 3 grams of water, so the loss of 1 pound of muscle glycogen in the average person results in about a 3-5 pound loss in weight. When glycogen stores are depleted, the body starts breaking down protein or lean muscle tissue to glucose. You don't want to lose lean muscle, as this keeps you trim and taut and also helps you burn calories fast. Fat will only be burned slowly so expect to lose only 1-2 pounds each week.

Crash diets can be boring, involve a limited number of foods, don't fit in with family meals and certainly play havoc with your social life – it's often a case of being housebound or eating nothing when out. You'll feel deprived and the temptation to break out will strengthen.

Crash diets don't change your eating habits. Once you've lost weight you must keep it off, so ideally a diet should teach you a better way of eating. Crash diets mean you'll return to your previous eating habits and the weight piles on again. A yo-yo or see-saw pattern of weight loss and weight gain results from this which is damaging for both your health and your self esteem.

Crash diets are often nutritionally un-balanced, being deficient in carbohydrates, dietary fiber, vitamins, minerals and, of course, calories. The small amount of food allowed results in you being tired and light-headed with less energy to expend on exercise.

DANGERS OF CRASH DIETS

Because crash diets are often nutritionally unsound they should not be followed for periods longer than 1 to 2 weeks without medical supervision.

Low-carbohydrate diets in particular result in ketosis (an accumulation of fatty substances in the blood) and cause other side-effects such as dizziness, dehydration, high cholesterol levels, constipation and kidney problems.

Deaths from heart failure have occurred due to the abuse of high-protein supplements (liquid or powder). These products are composed of protein and protein hydrolysates and lack other essential nutrients.

Fasting for too long without medical supervision can lead to an anorexic state and even result in death.

A general feeling of being unwell, both physically and psychologically, which can affect your everyday activities.

WHAT TO LOOK FOR WHEN A NEW DIET APPEARS

Does the diet:

☐ Make extravagant claims about losing weight quickly and effortlessly?

☐ Include very high-fat foods with little carbohydrate and fiber foods?

☐ Have limited choice of foods?

☐ Use exercise machines, rather than encouraging you to exercise?

☐ Require you to buy special diet supplements or pills and potions?

☐ Allow you to eat as much as you like of any one food and not put on weight?

☐ Highlight the particular importance of one food in the diet giving it "miracle" properties?

☐ Emphasize the importance of combining foods, i.e. one food should not be eaten with another?

If the answer to any of these questions is YES, then this is not a sound diet. Give it a miss!

FASTING

Fasting is a form of starvation or semi-starvation and is not recommended except under medical supervision. It is only used for very obese people (at least 50 pounds overweight) who have not been successful losing weight by normal means.

Hazards associated with fasting include nausea, dizziness, muscle cramps, vomiting, dehydration, bad breath, respiratory infections, constipation and menstrual cycle irregularities. Death can result.

If you are slightly overweight, fasting will only lead to a loss of water and muscle, not fat. Fasting does nothing for long-term weight loss.

FAD DIETS AND FAVORITES

Diets are great sellers of magazines, newspapers and books, so we are continually reading headlines about the latest fad diets. Below is a brief summary of the diets that work and the diets that fail which have been widely promoted.

HIGH-FIBER DIETS

High fiber diets are based on the theory that fiber is "roughage" – it is supposed to bulk up your stomach and pass through undigested, thus providing no calories. Unfortunately, latest research shows that certain fiber components are, in fact, digested, if not by human digestive enzymes then by bacteria which reside in our lower bowel. Nonetheless, as high-fiber diets tend to be correspondingly low in fat, coupled with the fact that fiber does require more chewing, these diets are in the main to be recommended.

☐ F-Plan Diet
☐ Save Your Life Diet
☐ Pritikin Diet

SINGLE-FOOD DIETS

Diets based on one food or food type (such as fruit only) claim that the particular food has a magical ability to speed up the body's metabolism and burn off fat. Others offer you "unlimited" quantities of a food – "as much as you can eat" – knowing that you will quickly get sick and tired of the same food and certainly reduce your total calorie intake. Boredom is their main feature, but many of them are too low in calories (adversely affecting metabolic rate) and deficient in basic nutrients. Followed for a week or less, they probably do little harm but are not recommended for serious dieters.

☐ The Grapefruit Diet
☐ The Spinach Diet
☐ The Airline Steward's Diet (6 hard-cooked eggs and white wine each day)
☐ The Israeli Army Diet
☐ The Beverley Hills Diet
☐ Day-On, Day-Off, Bread Diet
☐ The Egg Diet
☐ Bananas and Milk Diet
☐ The Rice Diet
☐ The Yogurt Diet

LOW-CARBOHYDRATE DIETS

Diets that eliminate bread, potatoes, pasta and sugary foods tell you that carbohydrates are the cause of all obesity. Avoiding carbohydrates puts the dieter in the wondrous state of ketosis, when the body is eliminating fat (in reality, accumulating fats are circulating in the blood and spilling over into the urine, as shown by ketone sticks). No-carbohydrate means a diet of meat, cheese, fish, mayonnaise, butter and cream, which creates a high-fat, high-cholesterol regime – hardly good fare for the heart. Other side-effects are nausea, constipation, tiredness and dehydration. The high weight loss on such diets is largely water and will return once carbohydrates are (eventually) eaten. Boring and hazardous, avoid all these diets.

☐ Dr. Atkins' Diet Revolution
☐ The Scarsdale Medical Diet
☐ Dr. Stillman's Quick Weight Loss Diet
☐ Boston Police Diet
☐ The Drinking Man's Diet
☐ The Woman Doctor's Diet

DIETS NOT RECOMMENDED

☐ Dr. Atkins' Diet Revolution
☐ Beverley Hills Diet
☐ Cambridge Diet
☐ Complete Scarsdale Medical Diet
☐ Cellulite Diet
☐ Drinking Man's Diet
☐ Formula Diet Drinks/Biscuits/Formulas
☐ The Israeli Army Diet
☐ Grapefruit Diet
☐ Egg Diet
☐ Dr. Fran's No Aging Diet
☐ High Sexuality Diet
☐ Fit For Life
☐ Fasting

THE IDEAL DIET FOR YOU...

✧ Must be nutritionally balanced including a variety of nutritious foods such as breads and cereals, fruit and vegetables, lean meat and dairy products, with limited quantities of butter, margarine or oils.
✧ Is moderate in energy – between 1000 and 1500 calories a day.

✧ Allows a modest weight loss of 1 to 2 pounds per week – this is fat, not water loss.
✧ Is flexible and varied, which fits in with your lifestyle and family.
✧ Can be followed for long periods of time.
✧ Uses ordinary foods and does not require special diet foods exclusively.

WEIGHING UP
THE DIETS

All diets carry a list of forbidden foods such as butter, margarine, cream, fried foods, nuts, fatty meats, plus their own particular food and food combination quirks.

❖

HIP AND THIGH DIET

Rosemary Conley's *Hip and Thigh Diet* promises to shed inches from areas of the body always difficult to slim, namely hips and thighs. It claims we can spot-reduce our bodies and lose "inches as well as pounds." There is no need to count calories or fat units – simply select one meal from the Breakfast, Lunch and Dinner menus listed (restricting red meat consumption to just two helpings a week) and keep to 1 cup skim milk per day.

The meals are very low in fats – both polyunsaturated and saturated. This will certainly help excess flab disappear, but not necessarily from the fattest parts of your body! Instead you may find you lose weight from all over, which is the single criticism of the book. But obviously the title has given it instant appeal, with sales of over 400,000 in the UK alone.

Rosemary Conley has been in the slimming business for 15 years, founding and running diet clubs and writing books on slimming. She stumbled on her new diet plan in 1986 when trying to avoid gallbladder surgery and was surprised to find herself with much slimmer hips and thighs. She later trialed the low-fat plan on 120 people for 8 weeks and reported that 98 of them had lost inches from trouble spots.

Overall, the diet is balanced and in tune with current nutrition guidelines, with a selection of quick, yet interesting, recipes to get you started. It won't do any harm, but don't be disappointed if it doesn't work on your specific problem spots.

TYPICAL MENU
Eat 3 meals a day (no snacks). One cup skim milk is allowed per day.

Breakfast
Select from:
☐ Cereal made with water, served with milk from allowance and two teaspoons of honey.

☐ Five prunes plus a natural yogurt.

Lunch
Select from:
☐ Baked potato topped with 8-oz. can baked beans.
☐ Four to five pieces of any fresh fruit.
☐ Jumbo sandwiches made with 4 slices wholewheat bread thinly spread with low-fat spread and filled with salad – lettuce, cucumber, cress, tomatoes, sliced Spanish onion, beets, peppers.

Dinner
Select one starter, one main course and dessert.

Starters
☐ Wedge of melon
☐ Half a grapefruit
☐ Clear soup

Main courses
☐ 8-oz. steamed, grilled or microwaved white fish served with unlimited boiled vegetables
☐ Chicken curry with boiled brown rice (recipe provided)
☐ 6-oz. chicken (no skin) steamed, grilled, baked or microwaved and served with unlimited vegetables

Desserts
☐ Sliced banana topped with raspberry yogurt
☐ Stuffed apple served with plain yogurt
☐ Strawberries served with strawberry yogurt
☐ Pears in red wine (recipe provided)

❖

FIT FOR LIFE

One of the most popular diet books, *Fit for Life* has come under criticism from professional dietitians the world over. Written by Harvey and Marilyn Diamond, it is based on the principles of Natural Hygiene and emphasizes "energy" and "vital forces of life". Food must be "properly combined" at a meal, so that proteins and starches are never eaten together, as the body cannot digest these two foods together. Thus lunch can be a salad with bread (but no cheese or meat), while dinner can be a large steak and vegetables (without a potato).

The body is supposed to undergo three cycles each day. From noon to 8 p.m. is our "appropriation" cycle, when eating should take place; from 8 p.m. to 4 a.m. is our "assimilation" cycle for absorption of previously-eaten food; and from 4 a.m. to noon is the "elimination" cycle when the body gets rid of wastes. The book claims that you will lose weight only when you "unblock the elimination cycle" (which detoxifies the body of its so-called wastes) and combine foods correctly.

You can only eat fruit on an empty stomach or else wait two to four hours after a meal, otherwise the fruit "spoils whatever is in the stomach". Breakfast consists of fresh fruit and juice (in any quantity) and no other food can be consumed before noon.

Fit for Life promises more energy, easy weight loss and better health, but there are so many rules of what and when to eat that most people who try the diet end up eating very little – which explains why there are reports of successful weight loss. The book makes no biological sense while appearing quite scientific to those with no knowledge of nutrition. The program is difficult to follow and ignores current concepts of a "balanced diet".

TYPICAL MENU

Breakfast
Eat fruit throughout the morning as you feel hungry.
Eat melons before other fruit.
Eat bananas if particularly hungry.
Start with fresh fruit juice if desired (up to 14 oz.)

Lunch

Fruit juice or fresh carrot juice, if desired. Energy salad consisting of different lettuces (iceberg, butter, romaine), spinach, cucumber, tomato, sprouts and any other raw vegetables, with olives and sesame seeds.

Properly combined sandwich made with 2 slices wholegrain bread (lightly toasted), spread with mayonnaise, mustard or butter and topped with tomato slices, cucumber slices, avocado slices, lettuce or sprouts.

Dinner

Freshly-squeezed mixed-vegetable drink
Cauliflower soup
Baked potato boats with squash and herbed stuffing
Roast chicken
Garlic green beans
Tossed green salad with olive oil and lemon juice

PRITIKIN

There are a number of variations of the popular Pritikin Program, all of which are very low in fat and cholesterol, high in unrefined carbohydrates, with no salt, sugar, coffee, tea or alcohol allowed. Your meals are based on vegetables, salads, wholewheat pasta and bread (but no butter or margarine permitted), brown rice and potatoes, but a tiny 3 ounces of fish, chicken or meat is allowed each day. Pritikin suggests that animal foods are regarded more as a garnish than the centre of the plate.

The Pritikin diets are regarded as unnecessarily severe and extreme by many health professionals. No fats of any kind are permitted in cooking and often the sheer bulk of high-fiber vegetables and grains is difficult to consume. Unless highly motivated, most people find them difficult to stick to and eating out is almost impossible.

Pritikin published a special version of his diet for slimmers. The Maximum Weight Loss diet has a very low 600 calories a day, which promises to get weight off quickly, if you follow it strictly.

You can eat as much of cooked and raw vegetables and vegetable soups as you like (packing a plastic bag full of raw vegetables to stave off hunger pangs during the day) plus one serving of dairy foods, grains and fruit allowed per day. As expected, it is low in fat, cholesterol and salt, but can be short in essential minerals like calcium, iron and zinc. If you do embark on it, don't follow it for any great length of time.

The Pritikin Program for Health and Longevity is a better balanced diet and a better choice for slimmers. With the many Pritikin-based cookbooks and food products now available, many people have incorporated low-fat recipes and cooking methods into their meals and found a healthier enjoyable way of eating. Despite its severity, Pritikin has made many aware of the need to reduce fats, cholesterol, salt and sugar.

TYPICAL MENU

Breakfast

Whole orange or half a grapefruit
Bowl of steaming hot wholegrain cereal (rolled oats, wheatgerm)
Skim milk
Pritikin wholemeal bread or toast, no butter or margarine

Lunch

Hearty bean and vegetable soup
Large mixed raw vegetable salad with oil-free dressing
Crusty wholewheat bread or crackers
Piece of fresh fruit

Dinner

Steamed vegetables (with a little lean meat, chicken or fish, if desired) over a mound of brown rice
Piece of fresh fruit

Snacks

Choose bread and crackers (unbuttered), fresh vegetables for munching, fresh fruit

WEIGHT WATCHERS

The longest running weight loss program in the world, the Weight Watchers diet is one of the most moderate and balanced in terms of calorie level, food choice, menu plan and nutritional value. It offers three sensible meals and snacks which total around 1200 calories for women and meets the recommended dietary intake for all nutrients.

Like other diets, fats, sugar and alcohol are restricted, but not eliminated completely. You choose foods by a food exchange system from breads and starchy foods, protein foods, fruits, dairy foods, non-starchy vegetables, fats, and optional extras. This allows flexibility and swapping of one food for another, so that instead of a slice of bread, you can substitute $^1/_2$ cup rice or one 3-ounce potato or $^1/_2$ cup spaghetti.

Weight Watchers' greatest appeal is its support system of regular weekly meetings led by group leaders who have successfully lost weight themselves. A group of people battling the same problem of excess weight can provide encouragement and "peer pressure" to keep even the most unmotivated dieter on the right track. Founded by Jean Neiditch (a housewife who enlisted friends to lose weight together) more than 20 years ago in the United States, Weight Watchers is now an international organization with classes held in 25 countries. Many other slimming groups have tried to copy its formula for success but none has done as well.

The emphasis is on balanced meals that all the family can eat, with exercise, behavior modification and group support. A gradual weight loss of half to 1 to 2 pounds a week is recommended, although there is a lower calorie diet for greater weight loss in the first few weeks.

TYPICAL MENU
Week 1 Quick success program

Breakfast

$^1/_2$ medium grapefruit
1 egg
1 slice toast spread with 1 teaspoon polyunsaturated margarine
$^1/_2$ cup skim milk
Coffee or tea, if desired

Lunch

1 ounce skinless chicken with lettuce and tomato made into a sandwich
1 small apple
Water, mineral water or low-calorie drink

Dinner

3 ounces fish fillet, baked, steamed or grilled
1 cup broccoli
Mixed green salads (2 cups) with no-oil salad dressing
$^1/_2$ cup skim milk

Snacks

1 medium peach
1 cup skim milk

WEIGHTY MATTERS

Although most authorities say that your weight should remain the same throughout your adult years, both women and men tend to gain weight after their 30s. The average person gains 7 pounds between his or her 25th and 35th birthday, but a small percentage put on much more than this (which raises blood pressure and cholesterol levels). But once past the age of 55, a new study shows that the pounds start to drop off, with women losing more than men.

SLIMLINE
DESSERTS

*Our light, luscious and refreshing selection
of dessert recipes will satisfy any cravings for something sweet
and keep you slim and healthy.*

❖
STRAWBERRY LIQUEUR FLAN

If you prefer, you can increase the orange juice to 2 tablespoons and leave out the Cointreau.

Serves 8

BASE
- ☐ **1 sheet prepared sweet shortcrust pastry**

LIQUEUR FILLING
- ☐ **1 cup ricotta cheese**
- ☐ **1/2 cup (low-fat plain yogurt**
- ☐ **3 tablespoons sugar**
- ☐ **1 tablespoon grated orange rind**
- ☐ **1 tablespoon orange juice**
- ☐ **1 tablespoon Cointreau**
- ☐ **3 teaspoons gelatin**
- ☐ **2 egg whites**
- ☐ **1 cup strawberries, halved**

GLAZE
- ☐ **3 tablespoons sugar-free apricot jam**
- ☐ **2 teaspoons Cointreau**

1　Line a lightly greased 9-inch flan dish with pastry. Trim edges and prick the bottom. Bake blind at 425° for 10 minutes, then reduce temperature to 350°. Remove blind bake and cook 10-15 minutes longer until light golden brown. Cool on a wire rack.

2　To make filling, place ricotta cheese, yogurt, sugar and orange rind in a food processor or blender and process until smooth. Transfer mixture to a mixing bowl. Fill a small bowl with hot water. Combine orange juice and liqueur in another small bowl. Sprinkle gelatin over and place on hot water bowl until gelatin dissolves. Cool gelatin mixture for 5 minutes then stir into cheese mixture.

3　Beat egg whites until soft peaks form and fold lightly into cheese mixture. Spoon filling into prepared pan and arrange strawberries decoratively over top.

4　To make glaze, place jam and liqueur in a small saucepan and cook over low heat, stirring constantly until jam melts. Push jam through a sieve until smooth and cool slightly. Brush fruit topping with glaze and refrigerate flan until firm.

258 calories per serving

Fat	*9.8 g*	*low*
Cholesterol	*22 mg*	*low*
Fiber	*6.0 g*	*high*
Sodium	*215 mg*	*low*

❖
SUMMER'S DAY FREEZE

Serves 4

- ☐ **1/2 cup sugar**
- ☐ **1/2 cup water**
- ☐ **1 tablespoon brandy**
- ☐ **2 cups unsweetened apple juice**
- ☐ **2 tablespoons finely chopped fresh mint**
- ☐ **1 egg white**

1　Combine sugar, water and brandy in a saucepan and cook over medium heat, stirring constantly until sugar dissolves. Bring to boiling, then reduce heat and simmer, without stirring, for 5 minutes until mixture thickens. Cool to room temperature.

2　Place apple juice and mint in a bowl and whisk in cooled syrup. Pour mixture into a shallow 9-inch square cake pan. Cover with aluminum foil and freeze until set.

3　Beat egg white until stiff peaks form. Break up frozen mixture with a fork and fold in egg white. Return mixture to shallow cake pan, cover with foil and freeze for several hours until set.

170 calories per serving

Fat	*0 g*	*low*
Cholesterol	*0 mg*	*low*
Fiber	*0.1 g*	*low*
Sodium	*30 mg*	*low*

❖
LEMON AND PASSIONFRUIT CREAM

Serves 4

- ☐ **1-ounce packet sugar-free lemon gelatin crystals**
- ☐ **1/2 cup boiling water**
- ☐ **3 tablespoons cold water**
- ☐ **1 cup evaporated skim milk, chilled**
- ☐ **pulp of 2 passionfruit**
- ☐ **lemon rind strips and passionfruit pulp for garnish**

1　Combine gelatin and boiling water in a bowl and stir until gelatin dissolves. Blend in cold water and set aside.

2　Beat skim milk in a bowl with electric mixer until thick. Fold in dissolved gelatin and passionfruit. Spoon into dessert dishes and chill until set. Garnish with strips of lemon rind and passionfruit pulp.

72 calories per serving

Fat	*0 g*	*low*
Cholesterol	*2 mg*	*low*
Fiber	*2.1 g*	*medium*
Sodium	*120 mg*	*low*

❖
APRICOT AND ORANGE MOUSSE

Serves 4

- ☐ **1 1/4 cups apricot nectar**
- ☐ **2 teaspoons superfine sugar**
- ☐ **1 teaspoon grated orange rind**
- ☐ **3 teaspoons gelatin**
- ☐ **4 tablespoons orange juice**
- ☐ **3/4 cup evaporated skim milk, chilled**

1　Combine apricot nectar, sugar and orange rind. Fill a small bowl with hot water. Place orange juice in another small bowl and sprinkle gelatin over. Place on bowl of hot water and stir until gelatin dissolves. Cool gelatin mixture for 5 minutes then stir in apricot mixture.

2　Beat skim milk in a bowl with electric mixer until thick. Fold into apricot mixture, spoon into dessert dishes and refrigerate until set.

131 calories per serving

Fat	*0 g*	*low*
Cholesterol	*2 mg*	*low*
Fiber	*0.1 g*	*low*
Sodium	*95 mg*	*low*

Strawberry Liqueur Flan, Lemon and Passionfruit Cream, Apricot and Orange Mousse and Summer's Day Freeze

HAZELNUT TORTE

Serves 8

- ☐ **4 egg whites**
- ☐ **3 tablespoons superfine sugar**
- ☐ **3 egg yolks**
- ☐ **$^1/_2$ cup ground hazelnuts**
- ☐ **4 tablespoons water cracker crumbs**
- ☐ **$^1/_2$ teaspoon baking powder**
- ☐ **1 teaspoon grated orange rind**
- ☐ **$^1/_4$ teaspoon almond extract**
- ☐ **1 cup strawberries, hulled**
- ☐ **1 teaspoon IOX (confectioner's) sugar**

1   Beat egg whites until soft peaks form. Add sugar a spoonful at a time, beating well after each addition until whites are thick and glossy.
2   Whisk egg yolks until light and fluffy, then stir in combined nuts, crumbs, baking powder, orange rind and almond extract.
3   Fold beaten egg whites into hazelnut mixture and spoon into a lightly greased and lined 9-inch springform cake pan. Bake at 350° for 30-35 minutes. Stand 5 minutes before turning out on a wire rack to cool.
4   When cool, decorate top of cake with strawberries and dust with IOX sugar.

167 calories per serving

Fat	8.9 g	low
Cholesterol	73 mg	low
Fiber	1.8 g	medium
Sodium	66 mg	low

SPICY APPLE CAKE

Serves 12

- ☐ **3 tablespoons polyunsaturated oil**
- ☐ **$^3/_4$ cup superfine sugar**
- ☐ **2 eggs, lightly beaten**
- ☐ **1 teaspoon vanilla extract**
- ☐ **1 cup self-rising flour, sifted**
- ☐ **1$^1/_2$ teaspoons apple pie spice**
- ☐ **12-ounce can unsweetened sliced apples, drained**
- ☐ **1 teaspoon grated lemon rind**
- ☐ **$^1/_2$ cup sultanas**

1   Combine oil and sugar in a large bowl. Whisk in eggs and vanilla. Combine flour and spice in one bowl and apples, lemon rind and sultanas in another. Fold flour mixture and apple mixture alternately into beaten egg mixture.
2   Spoon mixture into a greased and lined 9-inch ring pan and bake at 350° for 30-35 minutes or until cooked. Stand 5 minutes before turning out on a wire rack to cool.

159 calories per serving

Fat	3.5 g	low
Cholesterol	41 mg	low
Fiber	1.5 g	medium
Sodium	130 mg	low

BLUEBERRY AND APPLE CRUNCH

Serves 6

- ☐ **12-ounce can blueberries, drained**
- ☐ **12-ounce can unsweetened sliced apples, drained**
- ☐ **2 teaspoons grated lemon rind**
- ☐ **1 tablespoon butter, melted**
- ☐ **1 tablespoon brown sugar**
- ☐ **1$^1/_2$ cups cornflakes**
- ☐ **1 tablespoon sesame seeds**

1   Combine blueberries, apples and lemon rind and spoon into an ovenproof dish.
2   Mix together butter, sugar and cornflakes and spread over apple mixture in dish. Sprinkle sesame seeds over and bake at 350° for 20 minutes or until golden brown.

115 calories per serving

Fat	2.4 g	low
Cholesterol	6 mg	low
Fiber	3.8 g	high
Sodium	91 mg	low

Above: Spicy Apple Cake and
Hazelnut Torte
Right: Blueberry and Apple Crunch

GRAPEFRUIT AND PINEAPPLE SORBET

Serves 6

- ☐ **1 grapefruit, segmented**
- ☐ **2 slices ripe pineapple, peeled, cored and cubed**
- ☐ **3 cups apple juice**
- ☐ **1 tablespoon lemon juice**
- ☐ **¹/₂ cup fresh mint leaves**
- ☐ **3 egg whites**

1　Puree grapefruit, pineapple, apple juice, lemon juice and mint leaves in a food processor. Pour mixture into a shallow 11 x 7-inch cake pan. Cover with aluminum foil and freeze for 1 hour or until partly set.
2　Transfer fruit mixture and egg whites into a food processor and process until smooth. Return to shallow cake pan. Cover with foil and freeze for several hours or until set.

66 calories per serving

Fat	*0 g*	*low*
Cholesterol	*0 mg*	*low*
Fiber	*1.1 g*	*medium*
Sodium	*50 mg*	*low*

ORANGES IN LIQUEUR WITH CINNAMON-YOGURT SAUCE

If you find that your oranges are very sweet, leave out the brown sugar.

Serves 4

- ☐ **6 oranges, segmented**
- ☐ **3 tablespoons Grand Marnier**
- ☐ **2 tablespoons brown sugar**
- ☐ **¹/₄ teaspoon ground cloves**

CINNAMON-YOGURT SAUCE
- ☐ **1 cup low-fat plain yogurt**
- ☐ **1 tablespoon sugar**
- ☐ **¹/₂ teaspoon ground cinnamon**
- ☐ **pinch ground nutmeg**

1　Place orange segments in a dish with any juice collected in preparation. Combine Grand Marnier, sugar and cloves and drizzle over oranges. Cover and refrigerate for several hours or overnight, turning oranges in marinade occasionally.
2　To make sauce, blend together yogurt, sugar, cinnamon and nutmeg. Serve oranges in dessert dishes, topped with sauce.

196 calories per serving

Fat	*0.8 g*	*low*
Cholesterol	*4 mg*	*low*
Fiber	*5.8 g*	*high*
Sodium	*52 mg*	*low*

STRAWBERRIES AND KIWI FRUIT IN WINE

Serves 6

- ☐ **1¹/₂ cups strawberries, hulled**
- ☐ **3 kiwifruit, peeled and sliced**
- ☐ **1 tablespoon superfine sugar**
- ☐ **¹/₂ cup orange juice**
- ☐ **1 teaspoon grated orange rind**
- ☐ **¹/₂ teaspoon grated lemon rind**
- ☐ **1¹/₂ tablespoons Grand Marnier**
- ☐ **3 tablespoons Moselle wine**

1　Combine strawberries, kiwifruit, sugar, orange juice, orange rind, lemon rind, Grand Marnier and Moselle in a large glass bowl. Toss lightly to mix.
2　Cover fruit mixture and refrigerate for 2-3 hours, or until well chilled. Serve in glass dessert dishes.

63 calories per serving

Fat	*0 g*	*low*
Cholesterol	*0 mg*	*low*
Fiber	*2.6 g*	*medium*
Sodium	*8 mg*	*low*

❖
SPICED PRUNE AND APRICOT COMPOTE

Serves 6

- [ ] **12 pitted prunes**
- [ ] **12 dried apricots**
- [ ] **¹/₂ cup raisins**
- [ ] **12 dried apple rings**
- [ ] **4 whole cloves**
- [ ] **1 small cinnamon stick**
- [ ] **1 teaspoon grated lemon rind**
- [ ] **2 teaspoons finely chopped crystallized ginger**
- [ ] **³/₄ cup ginger wine**
- [ ] **³/₄ cup water**

Left: Strawberries and Kiwifruit in Wine, Oranges in Liqueur and Cinnamon Sauce and Grapefruit and Pineapple Sorbet
Below: Spiced Prune and Apricot Compote

GINGER DRESSING
- [ ] **1 cup low-fat plain yogurt**
- [ ] **1 tablespoon honey**
- [ ] **1 tablespoon finely chopped crystallized ginger**

1   Place prunes, apricots, raisins, apple rings, cloves, cinnamon stick, lemon rind, ginger, ginger wine and water in a saucepan and bring slowly to the boil.

2   Reduce heat and simmer, covered, for 10 minutes or until fruit is just tender. Cool and transfer to a serving dish. Cover and refrigerate for several hours or overnight.

3   To make dressing, blend together yogurt, honey and ginger. Just before serving, remove cloves and cinnamon stick from compote. Serve topped with ginger dressing.

137 calories per serving

Fat	0 g	low
Cholesterol	3 mg	low
Fiber	5.0 g	high
Sodium	46 mg	low

Cook's Tip

To bake blind, place pastry in flan dish. Line the pastry case with baking paper and weight down with uncooked rice, pasta or lentils. Bake blind for given time then remove paper and weights and continue to follow recipe. The rice, pasta or lentils can be stored and re-used again and again.

CLASSIC LIGHT

CREAMY CHEESECAKE

Serves 8

BASE
- [ ] ½ **cup cookie crumbs**
- [ ] **1 tablespoon ground hazelnuts**
- [ ] ¼ **cup (½ stick) butter, melted**

FILLING
- [ ] **1 cup ricotta cheese**
- [ ] ½ **cup cottage cheese**
- [ ] **1 tablespoon fine semolina**
- [ ] **2 tablespoons buttermilk**
- [ ] **3 eggs, separated**
- [ ] ¾ **cup superfine sugar**
- [ ] **2 teaspoons grated lemon rind**
- [ ] **3 tablespoons sultanas**

1 To make base, combine cookie crumbs, nuts and butter. Spread over the bottom of a lightly greased 9-inch springform pan and set aside.

2 To make filling, place ricotta, cottage cheese, semolina, buttermilk and egg yolks in a food processor or blender and process until smooth.

3 Beat egg whites until soft peaks form. Add sugar a spoonful at a time, beating well after each addition until whites are thick and glossy.

4 Fold cheese mixture into egg whites, then lightly fold in lemon rind and sultanas. Spoon mixture into prepared pan and bake at 350° for 50-55 minutes, or until firm. Cool in pan.

334 calories per serving

Fat	*16.0 g*	*medium*
Cholesterol	*130 mg*	*medium*
Fiber	*0.9 g*	*low*
Sodium	*221 mg*	*low*

HOW WE'VE CUT FAT AND CALORIES

✧ Instead of the usual cream cheese or cream cheese-and-yogurt combination, we have used ricotta cheese with cottage cheese and folded in beaten egg white to create a smooth creamy texture.

✧ Our crust has just enough butter to bind the bread crumbs. In its place you could use a sponge layer or low-fat pastry if preferred.

✧ Semolina thickens and sets the cake, reducing the need for another egg, so saving calories.

FACTS AND
FALLACIES

Most misunderstood foods for dieters.

GRAPEFRUIT
Often regarded as a "slimming" food with the power to "dissolve" unwanted flab, grapefruit have appeared on breakfast menus for dieters ever since the 1960s, when grapefruit diets first rose to popularity. The fruit's sour taste has no doubt contributed to this feeling, but it has no special slimming powers. Half a grapefruit supplies around 30 calories, the same as from half an orange. But, it is rich in vitamin C and fiber.

BREAD
Once banned from slimming diets entirely, bread is now regarded as a valuable food supplying satisfying carbohydrate, fiber and B vitamins. Sensible diets allow for at least 2 slices of bread a day, which should be wholewheat and mixed grain for maximum fiber. Often what is eaten with bread adds more calories than the bread itself. One slice of bread comes in at 63 calories, more for thick toasting bread, less for light protein-increased breads (once labeled as dieters' breads). Toasting does not reduce the calories.

ARTIFICIAL SWEETENERS
Sugar substitutes can be a useful aid for dieters wishing to satisfy a sweet tooth without piling on the calories. But, as they perpetuate a liking for sweetness, it is best to wean yourself off them eventually and develop a taste for less sweet foods. Saccharin and cyclamates have been in use for over 50 years and are 30 to 300 times sweeter than sugar without any calories. Saccharin's use is limited by its bitter metallic aftertaste, noticed more by some than others. Both sweeteners have come under fire for their long-term safety and cyclamates are banned in many countries.

Aspartame (Nutrasweet, Equal) is widely used to sweeten diet drinks, desserts and confectionery. Its excellent safety record and pleasant sugar-like taste have made it grow rapidly in popularity.

Acesulfame K is a new artificial sweetener recently approved as a tabletop sweetener and ingredient. Chemically similar to saccharin it is 200 times sweeter than sugar and its long-term safety is known. Unlike other sweeteners, it remains stable after heating, making it suitable for sweetening baked foods such as cakes and biscuits.

FIBER PILLS
Fiber supplements (tablets or powders) are designed to be taken with water before a meal to swell up in the stomach and create a feeling of fullness. Derived from cellulose, guar gum, glucomannan or mucilloid (plant gums), they are helpful for people who "tune in" to their body's signals of satiety and cease eating when full. But for dieters who overeat or binge-eat they are of no benefit. Fiber pills are expensive and are no substitute for food fiber if your diet is deficient. It would be cheaper and better for you to switch to more high-fiber foods instead.

Glucomannan in tablet form has been banned in some countries because it swells so quickly that it has been known to block the esophagus (the tube from the mouth to the stomach), almost causing death.

CIDER VINEGAR
Often promoted as a "slimming aid" by the health food industry, cider vinegar has no magical weight-dissolving properties. It is sometimes marketed in combination with kelp, vitamin B6 and lecithin as a diet supplement, but none of these have been scientifically proven to speed up weight loss. As vinegar has no calories, it is a harmless addition to a diet.

SLIMMER'S BISCUITS
Slimmer's biscuits, both savory and sweet are sold as a meal replacement for dieters. To lose weight, you simply replace two or three ordinary meals with biscuits (usually with a glass of milk). Such biscuits are not meant to be eaten as a snack or extra and have no weight-loss ability of their own. In fact, they often supply more calories than ordinary biscuits themselves.

Nutritionally they do not make a balanced meal, being high in sugar and fat with little fiber. Savory varieties contain less sugar, but more fat. A salad sandwich with a piece of fruit would be far healthier and less expensive. But for those dieters who wish to remove all temptations and are too busy to cook, slimmer's biscuits can provide a convenient occasional meal.

NUTRITION AND HEALTH

You cannot afford to skip the right foods because there's more to a balanced diet than just calories. Nutrition is vital to overall health, vitality, energy levels and your body's ability to fight infection. You cannot live in top gear on the wrong food. Here are guidelines from world nutrition authorities on how to plan a healthy balanced diet.

1   CUT BACK ON FAT

Excess fat is the major nutrition problem in most Western diets. It is related to many serious illnesses such as heart disease, gall bladder problems and certain types of cancer. It also leads to weight gain, as fat is calorie-laden, providing 37 calories per gram compared with 29 calories for alcohol and only 17 for carbohydrate and protein. Too much fat can make you fat!

Total avoidance of fat is neither wise nor desirable. A small amount is required by the body to provide essential fatty acids and fat-soluble vitamins A, D, E and K. But the quantity presently consumed by most people is too high for good health. Fat should constitute one-third or less of our daily calorie intake. Saturated fats found in fatty meats, butter, cream, solid cooking fats, most cheeses and many commercial foods (pies, fast food, pastries, biscuits and chocolate) tend to raise blood cholesterol and increase the likelihood of heart disesase.

Polyunsaturated fats have the ability to lower total cholesterol and are found in seed oils (safflower, sunflower, maize, cottonseed), polyunsaturated margarine and most nuts. Deep sea coldwater fish such as salmon, tuna, herring, ocean trout and mackerel are rich in omega-3 oils, unique polyunsaturated fats that researchers are now investigating for their ability to prevent heart disease and immunologically-related conditions.

Mono-unsaturated fats, concentrated in olive, peanut and grapeseed oils, as well as in avocados, were once thought to neither raise nor lower blood cholesterol. Now new research shows that they can lower the harmful LDL-cholesterol which contributes to fatty build-up on artery walls. Cholesterol is another fatty waxlike substance found in all animal foods – meat, poultry, fish, eggs and milk. It is essential for the production of hormones and the formation of cell walls.

Although most of the cholesterol in the body is manufactured by our livers, a high intake of cholesterol from food can raise blood cholesterol in some people. Such people either produce too much or do not get rid of it efficiently and need to avoid high cholesterol foods such as brains, kidney, liver, egg yolk and shrimp. But, it is far more important to reduce saturated fats than cholesterol, as excess of these "switches" on cholesterol synthesis.

2   EAT MORE FIBER

A healthy diet should include a range of fiber-rich foods from vegetables, dried beans, fruit, nuts, seeds to wholegrain cereals and wholemeal breads. Simply adding unprocessed wheat bran or oat bran to an otherwise ordinary diet does not confer all the benefits of fiber.

Fiber is nature's "appetite suppressant" and bulking agent. It creates a feeling of fullness and may put a brake on overconsumption – important for dieters. It also helps with bowel regularity, preventing constipation, hemorrhoids and possibly cancer of the bowel.

will not miss it after three to four weeks. More than 50% of our salt intake comes from commercial foods, so it is important to look for "salt reduced" and "no added salt" products when shopping. Low-salt cheese, bread, margarine, butter, snack foods, luncheon meats, canned foods and sauces are now readily available. Do not salt food for your baby or children.

5   EAT LESS SUGAR

Sugar supplies no other nutrients other than carbohydrate and can be eliminated from your diet without harm. On the other hand, small quantities improve the flavor and texture of certain dishes and can still be part of the balanced diet.

Remember that sugar in a sticky chewy form that clings to the teeth sets the scene for tooth decay. However, sugar dissolved in foods like soft drink and ice cream clears through the mouth quickly and so minimizes plaque build-up.

Three-quarters of our sugar intake is found in prepared foods such as soft drinks, cordials, confections, presweetened cereals, cookies, cakes and jams. Watch your intake of these if you are trying to eat for health.

Brown, raw and dark sugar, and honey are all forms of sugar. Although they contain tiny quantities of minerals and vitamins, the amounts present are not significant nutritionally.

Calories Supplied By Nutrients Per Gram	
Fat	37
Alcohol	29
Protein	17
Carbohydrate	16

Soluble fiber, found in oats, dried peas, beans, rice, barley and certain fruits, has the ability to remove cholesterol from the body. Unprocessed bran and other wheat products do not.

3   EAT MORE COMPLEX CARBOHYDRATES

Carbohydrates are the body's preferred source of energy, either in the form of blood glucose or as glycogen stored in the muscles or liver. Bread, potatoes, pasta and rice – excellent forms of complex carbohydrates – have often been maligned as "fattening". In fact, a slice of bread or a smallish potato has as few calories as an average apple! It is often the fat eaten with them that piles on the calories.

4   EAT LESS SALT

A high salt intake puts you at risk of hypertension (high blood pressure), a "silent disease" that not only contributes to heart attack but, if unchecked, can kill in its own right. Although some people can eat any amount of salt without ill effect, most of us need to minimize our salt intake. Heredity and obesity are two other factors to take into account.

Cut down on salt gradually in cooking and at the table and you

IS EATING MAKING
YOU FAT?

Ten foolproof tips to help you focus on bad eating habits – and break them. Gleaned from behavioral approaches to weight reduction, they have been successfully incorporated into many diet programs.

1 CHEW SLOWLY

If you demolish your meal in a hurry, the feeling of satisfaction will lag behind. Eating slowly allows more time for your stomach to signal the brain when full. So take smaller bites; chew each mouthful well; put fork and knife down between bites. Aim to be the last to finish, not the first.

2 SIT DOWN TO EAT

Most overeating is thoughtless eating – just a nibble as you walk by, an ice cream when shopping, some nuts in front of the television. Make yourself sit down, even if only to eat a snack. This helps you to concentrate on the food before you and to enjoy every calorie.

3 USE A SMALL PLATE

Forget large dinner plates. Serving food on a smaller plate – a simple eye trick – makes even a small portion look generous and not quite so miserable. Make food look as attractive as possible with presentation and garnishes.

4 KEEP FOOD OUT OF SIGHT

Store high temptation food in containers, in cupboards or at the back of the fridge. Don't leave nuts, fruit or sweets in bowls around the house. Often the mere sight of food triggers off hunger attacks (not true hunger).

5 DO NOTHING ELSE WHILE EATING

Do NOT read, watch television, write or talk on the telephone when you eat. You are likely to lose concentration and eat too much. Psychologists believe the two habits become "linked" in the mind, causing an automatic hunger, even after having eaten a meal. At work, if you can't leave your desk, clear a separate space on your desk at which to enjoy your lunch. Take 10 minutes off, relax and eat slowly.

6 DON'T HAVE TWO COMPETING PRESSURES

Don't start a diet when you are trying to break another habit or when a big decision is imminent. It's difficult enough to quit smoking or drinking without being on a diet; you probably won't have the strength to juggle the two. If you're starting a new job, if you're pregnant, if you're sick, if you're buying a house, moving house or getting divorced – these are not good times to start dieting.

7 DON'T SKIP MEALS

Strange as it sounds, this often leads to consuming more calories, not less! Feeling deprived usually leads

to making it up at the next opportunity. Especially with breakfast, the temptation for a morning tea of biscuits or cake is all too likely. It also slows your metabolism, making it harder to burn body fat.

8 REMOVE LEFTOVERS STRAIGHT AWAY

Clear the table after each meal and dispose of leftovers or put them immediately in the refrigerator. The time just after a meal is a vulnerable one for most people, so don't give yourself the opportunity to pick at uneaten food. Similarly don't nibble at your children's leftover foods – throw it out or else put it in a bowl for the dog.

9 KEEP BUSY

The busier you are, the less time you'll have to be tempted to overeat. Find activities or things to do that keep you away from the kitchen and occupy your hands – sewing, knitting, gardening, typing, doing a crossword, writing a letter and especially hobbies that require clean, unsticky hands such as cross-stitch, sewing or drawing. Seek out activities that are pleasant and absorbing.

10 STOP NEGATIVE THINKING

Don't feel sorry for yourself and think "It's not fair that I have to watch what I eat". Catch yourself if you start imagining the pleasure you once might have got from certain foods. Instead enjoy your abstinence and better health. Think "one day at a time"; forget about yesterday's cravings or the possibility of tomorrow's. Whenever you feel like a snack, stop yourself and replace that thought with another of yourself wearing something nice.

DIETER'S DOWNFALLS

☐ Nibbling while cooking
☐ Polishing off the kid's leftovers
☐ Finishing the last cookie that won't fit in the cookie jar
☐ Tasting every dish while cooking
☐ Eating the last piece of cake because "it was there"
☐ Putting the diet off for another day

PAMPER YOURSELF

☐ Take a long bubble bath.
☐ Treat yourself to a facial. It will cleanse and rejuvenate your skin and make you feel good.
☐ Reward yourself every day or so with a special treat – a new glossy magazine, a lipstick, a bunch of flowers, a special coffee mug.
☐ Book a weekend at a health farm or spa.
☐ Go to a movie.
☐ Give your feet a pedicure. Soak feet in a bowl of warm water with bubble bath or body oil. Trim nails and apply nail polish if you wish. Ask your partner to massage your feet with oil or light cream.
☐ Have a long luxurious body massage – good for the body and the mind!
☐ Visit an art gallery.
☐ Buy that new record, tape or compact disk you've been wanting.

FOOD AND FEELINGS

Uncontrolled episodes of overeating or binge-eating are frequently the cause of excess weight and one of the major reasons why dieters "break their diet plan". It is essential to distinguish whether the bingeing is frequent and affecting your whole outlook on life or just simply an overindulgence when there was lots of good food. Some 40% of the population report that they binge-eat, but this does not cause guilt or a feeling of being "out of control" when around food.

If you feel food and eating are dominating your entire life, then embarking on a strict diet plan is not for you – it only serves to impose food limitations and prevents you discovering your own appetite and satiety patterns.

It is best to seek counseling to gain insight as to why you misuse food. Your local doctor, community nurse or social worker can advise you or else refer you to a trained counselor in eating disorders.

REV YOUR BODY AT A
HIGHER RATE

*Exercise burns up calories and raises your body's
metabolic rate for 24 to 48 hours afterwards. The important
thing is to find the sport you like which fits your lifestyle –
and do it regularly.*

CALORIE-BURNERS

LIGHT 2-5 cals burned per minute	MODERATE 5-8 cals burned per minute	HEAVY 8-10 cals burned per minute	VERY HEAVY 10 cals burned per minute
Walking, slow	Walking, fast	Jogging	Swimming, training
Bowling, lawn or ten-pin	Gardening, heavy	Skipping	Squash, advanced
Golf	Tennis	Country dancing	Cross-country skiing
Ping pong	Bicycling	Disco dancing	Marathon running
Housework, light	Horseriding	Aerobics	Rowing
Gardening, light	Skating	Downhill skiing	Basketball
Yoga	Swimming, moderate	Netball	Uphill hiking
Water skiing	Ballroom dancing	Football	Fast bicycling
Painting	Sailing	Hockey	
Carpentry	Surfing	Climbing stairs	
Light industry	Hiking		
Assembly work			
Clerical work			

For successful weight loss, you need to expend energy in a way that is "aerobic", that is any activity which increases the oxygen needs of the body, so exercising the heart and lungs. Exercises which use the large muscles of the body (thighs, trunk, shoulders) over an extended period are good forms of aerobic conditioning (see below). You should find an activity that is convenient, enjoyable and can be maintained for 30 minutes or more as a continuous movement. Start at a careful level and build up activity gradually, as you develop stamina and condition. Some people find motivation easier if they join a health club or gym; others prefer to set the alarm half an hour earlier, slotting their exercise in first thing in the morning. Whichever way, make sure you tailor exercise to your lifestyle and physical condition. If you are unfit, check with your doctor before undertaking vigorous exercise.

☐ Incorporate more activity into your life:

✧ Walk wherever you can, instead of driving or taking a bus.

✧ Climb up stairs, instead of taking the elevator.

✧ Hire an exercise bike; pedal while watching television or reading.

✧ Take the dog for a walk every day.

✧ Attack the housework with vigor and energy.

✧ Take regular short breaks at work to stretch and use inactive muscles.

✧ Go dancing at night; spend as much time as you can on the dance floor.

MUSCLE VERSUS FAT

When you exercise aerobically on a regular basis and follow a diet, you may find the scales show no weight loss at all or sometimes even a weight gain. Do not become discouraged. Muscle is heavier than fat and, as you lose body fat, you are replacing it with heavier muscle plus increasing your muscle-to-fat ratio. Rather than registering on the scales, it will show up in your measurements. It is best not to weigh yourself more than once a week; rely instead on the measuring tape and how your clothes fit.

TROUBLE SPOTS

It is impossible to remove fat from only one problem spot of the body – stomach, bottom, thighs – by exercising that area alone. Fat is lost from all over the body, not just the fattest part, so your overall proportions may remain the same. One weight loss expert has commented that large pears often slim into smaller pears! The best way to slim a flabby tummy or largish hips is by eating less (reducing the calories consumed) and/or by aerobic exercise (increasing the calories burnt up). The exercise may not even involve those parts of the body where trouble exists – have you ever seen a marathon runner with a fat stomach? With "spot" exercises, like sit-ups for the stomach, you may just end up with a tight fat stomach. The muscles underneath become tight, but the fat over the top remains there! You may still need to diet and start your whole body moving to shed the excess fat first. But if you have little fat covering your muscles, spot exercises can improve the shape of a particular muscle, resulting in lost inches and a tighter more contoured outline.

HOW EXERCISE HELPS

✧ Increases resting metabolic rate, which accounts for some 70% of calorie expenditure.
✧ Helps lower blood cholesterol, including a proportion of the dangerous LDL-cholesterol fraction.
✧ Helps reduce blood pressure in mildly hypertensive people.
✧ Reduces blood glucose levels and increases the effectiveness of insulin for diabetics.
✧ Improves muscle strength and joint flexibility, which helps fight osteoarthritis.
✧ Reduces the risk of bone fractures and development of osteoporosis in later life in women.
✧ Improves sleeping patterns.
✧ Can alleviate mild depression and tension, improve confidence.

WALKING

Walking is a good all-round exercise because it is convenient, requires no expensive equipment, can be done by anyone of any age without any special skill or training. It does less damage to joints and muscles than jogging, while still toning the heart and lungs. Walk at a pace that's fast enough so you can cover 3 to 4 miles in an hour. Step out in your stride and swing arms from side to side, thus ensuring that your torso, not just your lower body, becomes involved. Begin with short distances, especially if you're very overweight or sedentary. Aim to cover more distance at each walk, as research shows that people use almost the same calories walking a set distance, whether they walk it in 15 minutes or in 30!

JOGGING

Jogging or running has problems not associated with walking due to the occurrence of joint injury, sprained tendons or "shin splints" (painful bruising of the calf). Jogging is definitely not for the unfit or the very overweight. But, if you'd like to jog, start out with brisk walks interspersed with jogging to build up stamina. A modest 2-mile run each day will keep your body in good condition and can be accomplished in under half an hour.

You will need a pair of good running shoes, as ordinary sneakers do not provide enough support and cushioning. Try to jog on grass or soft dirt, as concrete causes high impact for joints. Always begin with five minutes of warm-up stretching exercises. Bouncing on a mini-trampoline gives you the benefits of running in the privacy of your home without the ill-effects of injuries or the vagaries of the weather.

Power walking for pleasure

SWIMMING

Swimming is a most refreshing and tension-draining form of exercise. It works the whole body without overstraining joints. As well as providing a good aerobic workout, swimming is excellent for toning many major muscles. Doctors recommend it for people with neck and back problems, as well as arthritis.

All strokes will improve your fitness. Overarm (crawl) and butterfly are the most demanding and burn up the most calories. Breast and side stroke, with their momentary pause between strokes, are less efficient, but nevertheless still good exercise.

Begin with one or two laps, followed by two minutes of rest, followed by more laps until you tire. Build up your stamina and capacity gradually until you are swimming 20 to 30 continuous Olympic-sized laps.

CYCLING

Cycling offers one of the best cardiovascular workouts, while burning calories and going places as well! A stationery exercise bike is a good buy for people with busy schedules, but you need the motivation to ride it regularly. Aim to cruise at about 6 miles per hour on level ground, using a bike with three speeds or less. If you own a 10-speed bicycle, just don't shift into an easier gear too often. Trained cyclists generally cover around 25 miles in 1½ hours which means traveling at a speed of 15 miles per hour. Riding uphill or against wind, pedalling faster or riding against resistance on an exercise bike will burn more calories.

AEROBICS SLIMNASTICS

Joining a fitness club or gymnasium for regular group classes is a time-efficient way to ensure you get your exercise in today's sedentary world. Start at the beginner's class to avoid muscle soreness and build up your attendance to three or four times a week. To avoid boredom, try various classes – low-impact aerobics (for fitness without jumping or jogging), stretch and tone classes (for specific muscle stretching) or circuit (where you move from machine to machine around the gym, interspersed with a minute's vigorous jogging or cycling to keep heart rate up). Follow the leader's instructions carefully and try to copy the exercise exactly to avoid injury.

Most women like to buy a leotard, tights and supported gym shoes, but shorts and a loose T-shirt plus jogging shoes or sneakers will do while you try out a few classes. Exercise classes can be boring and lonely, as busy people dash in and out for their post-work class. It helps to learn some of the routines, play some music and put them to work at home.

TENNIS/SQUASH AND OTHERS

Most social sports are less efficient at eliminating fat than the more demanding workouts from solo sports such as jogging, skipping with a rope or cross country skiing. But they are much more enjoyable and require less self-discipline. Squash obviously gives a better aerobic workout than tennis and playing singles requires more endurance than doubles. Squash also has its drawbacks because of the sudden bursts of activity that can place strain on an unfit heart.

The important thing is to find a sport you like which fits your lifestyle, and do it regularly (see Chart). Windsurfing (sailboard riding) strengthens muscles, yoga and gymnastics keep you flexible and supple, golf builds the shoulders and back muscles. Each sport has its own benefits. Remember it is safer and more beneficial in the long run to pay for proper instruction than to attempt to struggle on your own. It's also a good way to meet others interested in the sport and form your own network of sports partners.

CHOOSING A SPORT

Sport	Aerobic Fitness	Flexibility	Body Fat	Muscle Tone
Aerobics	8	8	8	8
Basketball	8	4	8	5
Cycling	8	1	6	5
Canoeing	7	3	5	6
Gymnastics	6	10	9	10
Hockey	7	4	8	5
Running	9	1	10	5
Skiing (Cross Country)	10	2	10	6
Squash	6	1	6	5
Swimming	7	3	1	7
Tai Chi	3	6	3	2
Tennis	5	4	6	5
Walking	4	2	7	3
Windsurfing	5	3	4	5

Each component is assessed on a scale of 1 to 10, with 10 being the maximum.

TIGHTEN AND TONE WITH
EXERCISE

Try these four easy exercises to tighten and tone your thighs and abdomen. All it takes is a few minutes everyday and you will feel trim, taut and terrific.

A INNER AND OUTER THIGHS

1 Stand tall with legs wide apart.
2 Bend knees, so they come directly above your feet.
3 Now, lower body, increasing bend, hold for 4 counts.
4 Slowly lift the body up again. Repeat until legs start to tire. Gradually work up to repeating the exercise 10 times.

B UPPER ABDOMEN

1 Lie flat on back with knees bent and feet flat on floor.
2 Breathe in. As you breathe out, lift your head and chest, reaching forward with hands towards knees.
3 Lower yourself gently to floor.
4 Repeat the whole exercise until you tire. Work up to 10 repetitions.
5 Repeat this routine, reaching forward with right hand to left knee. Repeat alternately 10 times.

C LOWER ABDOMEN

1 Lie on back, knees bent. Place hands under head.
2 Bring knees up and in towards head, while reaching forward with elbows to meet knees. Repeat until you tire, then work up to 20 repeats. A slow controlled movement is best.

D BOTTOM AND BACKS OF THIGHS

1 Kneel on all fours. Then place elbows on the floor, leaving your bottom up.
2 Push right knee up behind you in a donkey kick, keeping knee bent. Return to original starting position.
3 Repeat 5 times and then repeat exercise with other leg. Gradually work up to 10 repeats with each leg.

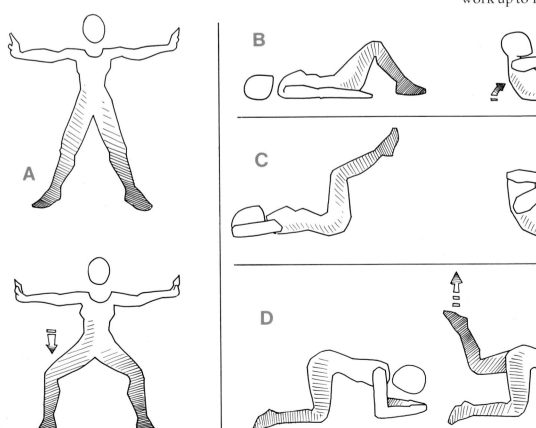

BODY LINES

The secret of well-dressed women is that they know how to highlight their best features and play down their weak points.

ALL ABOUT APPLES AND PEARS

Not all body fat is the same! The recent discovery that fat around your waist may be more dangerous than fat on your thighs and bottoms has astounded researchers in the field of obesity.

Being pear-shaped – having a big bottom, largish thighs and small breasts – is the last thing most women want to be. But researchers have found that pear-shaped women have a health advantage over their big-breasted, slim-legged sisters.

Excess fat distributed over hips and lower parts of the body is not linked with any major disease. Fat stored around the waist – spare tires and beer bellies – has been found to be associated with heart disease and diabetes. In other words, apple-shaped people are more prone to health problems than the pear-shaped.

Scientists are only beginning to understand the differences between "apples" and "pears". The abdominal fat on apple-shaped people appears to interfere with the breakdown of insulin, which could eventually lead to diabetes and high blood pressure. It also is more prone to store up high concentrations of fatty acids. These substances are released into the bloodstream, putting "top heavy" women at greater risk of developing illnesses like heart disease.

In contrast, fat stored on the thighs and hips is less metabolically active. Instead of being broken down quickly to circulate in the body, it tends to stay put until there's an urgent need for it. It is a most efficient way to store a deposit of energy for lean times and explains why pear-shaped women often find it virtually impossible to slim down their lower curves.

These new findings also explain why women who generally have fatter thighs or hips than men, have fewer heart attacks, despite being more overweight.

If pear-shaped means better health and longevity, it may again become a fashionable shape – as in the artist Rubens's time.

MALE VERSUS FEMALE FLAB

Why do women put on more weight than men? Leftover weight after pregnancy is often thought to be the reason, but now researchers feel it may be due more to physical activity – women tend to exercise less than men.

Women are also likely to go on and off diets and over the years, yo-yo dieting slows the body's metabolic rate. In addition to women's smaller proportion of lean muscle tissue, this drop in metabolism makes it harder to burn up calories. The solution is regular aerobic exercise which will replace unhealthy fat with metabolically active muscle and raise the metabolic rate – often for 24 hours after.

YOU CAN DRESS 5LB'S LIGHTER

Whatever your shape, there are many ways to make you look slimmer without even shedding an ounce! All it takes is clever use of styles and colors combined with a sense of balance and proportion when choosing clothes.

☐ Decide what's right for you. Be honest about your figure type (see following pages), then buy fashions to balance and flatter.

☐ Darker colors have a slimming effect; light bright colors make you look larger.

☐ Large bold patterns draw attention to large figures, while small and medium-sized patterns reduce the scale of your body.

☐ Vertical lines are, in general, slimming. But take care with very wide stripes which can attract the eye and look unflattering.

☐ Vertical lines do not have to be stripes. Pin tucks, front zippers, rows of buttons and gore skirts also create the illusion of vertical lines.

☐ Focus attention upwards with a colorful splash of a scarf, a pretty collar or eye-catching jewelery.

☐ Choose tights or pantyhose to match shoes – not your outfit – to make legs look longer.

☐ Wear an unbroken line over your largest part (a straight skirt over wide hips) to draw the eye away from that part.

☐ Invest in jackets and long cardigans. A jacket smooths over hips and bottoms and adds inches vertically. Left unbuttoned, it reveals a vertical "stripe" down the center of the body.

☐ Shoulder pads are wonderful for balancing out wider hips and thighs and enhancing a slim waist.

ROUND
- Broad shoulders and/or large bust
- Slim hips and legs
- An inverted triangle
- Can have heavy arms

Avoid
- Frills, gathers and ruffles on tops
- Pockets that draw attention to your top half
- Strapless or body-hugging tops
- Tight blouses and sweaters
- Cut-away shoulders and skimpy sleeve lines
- Light colors on top
- Chokers, necklaces, scarves close to the neck
- Puffed or dolman sleeves

SQUARE
- Squarish figure with only a slight body curve
- Can be tall, straight up and down or short and flattish
- Fat accumulates most often around the waist

Avoid
- High waists
- Straight dresses that hang from the shoulders
- Vertical stripes or pin tucks that emphasize lack of curves
- One-color looks

TRIANGLE
- The most common female shape
- Narrow shoulders, average waist, large hips, bottom and thighs
- Resembles a triangle with its peak at your shoulders

Avoid
- Short or cropped jackets
- Tight clingy blouses and sweaters
- Pockets on trousers or skirts
- Short straight skirts
- Light-colored trousers and skirts
- Horizontal lines on lower torso

Baklava
1
400 cals

Croissant
1
200 cals

DIETER'S
FOES

Foods that will wreck your diet

Pâté
1 tablespoon
55 cals

Margarine
1 teaspoon
35 cals

Toasted muesli
$^1/_2$ cup
135 cals

Stilton cheese
1 piece (1 oz.)
130 cals

Peanuts
2 oz. package
280 cals

Sesame bar
1 bar
170 cals

Peanut butter
1 tablespoon
170 cals

Mayonnaise
1 tablespoon
142 cals

Chocolate Bar
1 Mars bar
260 cals

Cream/sour cream
1 tablespoon
pouring 35% fat   73 cals
light 18% fat   36 cals
rich 48% fat   93 cals

Block chocolate
6 squares
160 cals

Potato chips
1 oz. package
150 cals

Bacon
1 slice fried
145 cals

Oil (all types)
1 tablespoon
176 cals

Chocolate cake
1 slice, $^1/_8$ of 10-inch cake
350 cals

Sausage roll
1 small
175 cals

French fries
20 medium
210 cals

Takeout fried chicken
Average piece
430 cals

Butter
1 teaspoon
35 cals

CHILD CARE
Q & A

Food for thought on overweight children.
Your questions answered.

Q Won't children grow out of their excess weight?

A Never dismiss overweight in children as just "baby fat". Fat children tend to grow into fat adults and many have high levels of blood fats or high blood pressure from a very early age. Children are especially vulnerable to becoming fat during the first six months of life and in early adolescence from ages 11 to 15. When children overeat at this time, the unused calories are used to make new fat cells. Once created, the number of fat cells remain unchanged for life, making it extremely difficult to lose weight later. So pay attention at these periods to children's eating habits and activity levels. In infancy, early introduction of solids and over-concentrated formulas are both considered to cause fatness in babies. During puberty, there are bewildering changes in body shape, emotions and other changes to contend with, triggering a need for solace and comfort, which food often satisfies. In addition, there are psychological problems – chubby children are prone to poor self-esteem and mild depression. They suffer teasing from other children, which only tends to make them seek comfort from food.

Q Should children be put on a low-calorie diet?

A Children are growing and require sufficient protein, calcium, vitamins and other essential nutrients each day. Overweight children should never be put on a strict diet for rapid weight loss. Rather, a sensible everyday food pattern is best. This aims to hold them at their present weight over a period of 6 to 12 months while their height increases to bring them into their ideal weight-for-height range.

Q What constitutes sound diet-type meals for children who are too fat?

A It is best if all the family eats similar meals. Low-fat, high-fiber dishes are good for everybody, not just those needing to shed weight. Try to prepare attractive food when trying to tempt children to eat new dishes. Breakfast can be a wholegrain cereal or rolled oats, followed by toast with a scrape of margarine or butter with peanut butter or cheese. If they are big milk drinkers, low-fat milks today taste excellent and help satisfy the appetite with less calories.

Pack a well-balanced lunch for your child to take to school, comprising a sandwich or roll filled with lean meat, chicken, baked beans, tuna and as much salad as they will accept. A piece of fruit or a carton of low-fat fruit yogurt completes the meal. Dinner should be a moderate serving of the family's meal with vegetables or raw vegetable sticks.

Q How can I ban snacks between meals?

A Snacks really are a part of children's eating patterns because of their smaller stomach capacity. Try to make the snacks more on the nutritious side – a wedge of cheese with crackers, bread spread with peanut butter or yeast extract, a piece of fresh fruit, cup of plain hot popcorn, wholewheat or plain biscuits, frozen fruit ices. Older children should be more able to accept three meals a day with no snacks in between.

Q How important is heredity in determining body weight and shape?

A Parents often excuse their child's excess weight as normal because it "runs in the family". Experts do not fully agree on whether our genes or our environment have the greatest influence on weight. A large study of adopted children in Denmark found that the size of the children consistently reflected the size of their natural parents. But while heredity can determine build, it cannot define the degree of body fat. If your child comes from a "big build" family, then try and neutralize any inherited tendency by regular eating habits and vigorous sport.

Q How can I make sure my child does not become fat?

A Prevention of overweight is much easier than the cure. Stick to the following guidelines to ensure your children do not become overweight.

• Try not to offer food as reward for good behavior. A major problem is food featured on television. Children see soft drinks, candy, cookies, heavily-sugared cereals, ice creams and salted snacks on the screen and demand them, wanting to be "like all the other kids".

• Set a good example yourself and keep "junk food" to a minimum or for outings or special occasions only.

• Encourage exercize and outdoor play rather than hours spent inactive in front of the television.

• Frequent illness in infancy often convinces parents that a child needs extra feeding, leading to weight problems later on. When children are sick, we tend to pamper them with treats to boost their spirits. Be aware of this when they return to better health.

• Insecurity and emotional problems are often causes of overeating. Perceived rejection from parents, rivalry, moving to a new neighborhood or school, feeling left out or unhappy are all triggers for the unhappy child to turn to food.

• Ban thoughtless snacking in front of television and don't let children wander around the house munching snacks.

• Explain your attitude to family and friends. It's tempting for grandparents and aunts to hand out sweets at every visit, but this is unhealthy in the long term.

INDEX

ACKNOWLEDGEMENTS
The publishers would like to thank Penelope Van Riet B Sc, Dip Nutrition & Dietetics, Consultant Dietitian; Garry Egger M PH, Ph D, CSCS, Health Promotion Consultant and McCalls "Clothes Sense" Palmer/ Pletsch for their assistance during production.

Active Service; Australia East India Company; Corso de Fiori; Country Farm; Dansab; Grace Bros, Chatswood; Lifestyle Imports; Made in Japan; Made Where; Mid City Home and Garden; Mikasa; People's Behaviour; Rebel Sports, Bondi Junction; Stewart James; The Bay Trees; Whitehouse Interior Design for their assistance during photography.

Admiral Appliances; Blanco Appliances; Master Foods of Australia; Meadow Lea Foods; Namco Cookware; Sunbeam Corporation Ltd.